To Fred,
Best Wishes
Ron (Binnie) Spyford
22.9.13
w/o Elliott 192 SQDN

THE ADVENTURES
OF
'BINKIE' BAYFORD

F/SGT Jimm cGillivray 115 SQN
REAR GUNNER LANCASTERS
AGE 18.

Ruth C. Smith

THE ADVENTURES OF 'BINKIE' BAYFORD

One Man's journey through WW2

Ron Bayford

Mitor Publications

Published & typeset by
Mitor Publications
20 Theydon Gardens,
Rainham,
Essex
RM13 7TU
www.mitorpublications.co.uk

ISBN 978-0-9557180-2-1

Cover design by Ian Taylor
ian.taylor21@sky.com

Printed by Berforts Information Press Ltd

CONTENTS

ACKNOWLEDGEMENTS

I wish to sincerely thank the following people who helped to bring my memories alive and this book to final fruition. To my publisher Richard C. Smith and his wife Kim, who spent many hours going through my original manuscript, and to their son Robert who finished the final edit, turning it into book form. Thanks to the Imperial War Museum, London, for allowing the use of photographs from their archive. The National Archive, Kew in London. Thanks also to David Brocklehurst and Mike Llewellyn of the Kent Battle of Britain Museum at Hawkinge in Kent for their assistance and John Davies of Grub Street Publishers for use of 91 Squadron pilot biographies. To photographer and designer Ian Taylor, for all his help in producing the book cover and photo section and Mr Jim Davies, for the excellent back cover photograph. Last, but by no means least, to Andrew MacKinlay, former MP of Thurrock, for his encouragement to get me to get my memoirs published.

INTRODUCTION

Over the past few decades, many times I have been asked 'What did you do during the war? And I tell them that I was in the Royal Air Force; the next question was always the same, 'Were you aircrew? I had to say that I was ground staff. The next remark was always the same 'Oh! Was that all! Yes, that was all, but what was all?

When the dust had settled at the end of the Second World War, there was a spate of books and films relating to deeds of individuals, units and commands of all three services. The Royal Air Force had more than its fair share of publicity, exploits of Fighter, Bomber and Coastal Command and even Air Sea Rescue. I read about these exploits and one day it occurred to me that nowhere was there any reference to the poor flippin 'erks' who worked and maintained the aircraft.

During the Battle of Britain, there were hundreds of these 'erks' who helped keep the aircraft serviceable and many were killed or wounded, when the Luftwaffe decided to eliminate our airfields. These unsung heroes were subject to bombing and strafing on a regular basis whilst refuelling and re-arming their aircraft between sorties. The Battle of Britain could not have been won if the 'erks' had bottled their duties. fitters, riggers, wireless mechanics, armourers, instrument 'Bashers' electricians and even the men who drove the petrol bowsers, worked on through the attacks, some paying the ultimate price for doing so. Even the WAAFs in the Control Room had their share of fatalities.

I was one of the lucky ones – I had nearly five years on the dispersals and know what it was like to be 'shot up' and bombed whilst servicing aircraft; but I came out unscathed except for a smashed knee, so I decided to put down on paper my own experiences, so for those who just say – 'Is that all!
This is a testimonial for my mates who did not make it and for those who did.

Ron 'Binkie' Bayford
March 2012

PROLOGUE

I am, always will be a patriot. Ever since I can remember I have always loved patriotic songs and literature.

At school every year, we celebrated Empire Day, Saint George's Day and the King's Birthday in Grays Park, where we would sing patriotic songs and play games. Those were the days and times when we were proud to be British. We had heroes and heroines to look up to, and show the rest of the world how great we were. There was the wonderful Amy Johnson, whose exploits flying round the world solo in her famous biplane, captured the hearts of the whole country. Add to this, Sir Malcolm Campbell broke the world speed record in his famous racing car 'Bluebird' and did the 'double' by breaking the speed record on the water in his speedboat.

The icing on the cake was when the Schneider Trophy was won outright for England by the Supermarine S6, from which the famous Spitfire was developed. I like to think that winning the trophy was behind my Father taking me to the RAF display at Hendon, where I was so thrilled; I made my mind up to join the Royal Air Force when I was old enough.

I was in my early teens when the Spanish Civil War broke out and was horrified, when the Germans decided to help the Fascists to bomb the unprotected towns and killed thousands of innocent civilians in the process. I was so angry that I went and joined the newly formed Air Raid Precaution Unit in Grays. There I learned about Mustard and Phosgene gases, high explosive and Incendiary bombs, basic first aid and procedures to be taken when air raids occurred.

In spite of all this, life went on as usual and in my spare time, in spite of the fact that I did not know the first thing about music, I taught myself to play the Piano, Ukulele, Banjo and Guitar. Although my elder brother and younger sister both learned music, I could never understand how to 'read the dots.' But somehow I learned to form chords and what they called them. I became accomplished enough to attract attention from local band leaders, and at the age of fourteen, I was playing in the local bands not by reading music, but reading the right chords at the right time. This stood me in good stead for years, even to the extent of sitting in with the Squadronaires, who at the end of a session, Jimmy Miller the band leader presented me with a signed piece of paper 'To Binkie from the Squads.' This memento is now in the hands of the present 'Squads' whom I met at a concert in 2006. Their leader told me it was a rarity to have the signatures of the whole band and it would be treasured by today's band.

At the outbreak of war, I reported to the ARP Headquarters in Grays and on the Sunday morning Major Hampson, head of the ARP instructed me to cycle down to Tilbury Ferry and help with the evacuation of children. When I arrived at the ferry, there were hundreds of mothers saying 'goodbyes' to their children who were boarding one of the three paddle steamers, to be evacuated to safety. It was heart breaking to see and help so many mothers saying their goodbyes.

After the ships had sailed, I reported back to headquarters; I was in the incident room when the telephone rang, I answered it, there was a message to say that the children were all safely at Clacton and would be 'fostered out.' I relayed the message to Major Hampson and he told me to get on my bike and ride round Grays town centre, shouting to the town's people that their children were safe.

It was a hectic life at the time, for I was at work from 8 am to 5.30 pm, home to tea, then off again on ARP until 7.00 am; then home again to wash, change for breakfast and off to work. Officially, I was the Incident Officers messenger, so I saw enough bomb damage to last a lifetime. To mention a few, I attended Shellhaven, Thameshaven, Jurgens, Esso, the Thames Board Mills and Shell at Purfleet; not to mention the private homes all over Thurrock.

On reflection I must say, I never gave a thought about my Mother's position. She must have worried every night wondering if I was alright. When I came home in the morning, she would say 'Alright Son? 'Go and wash and change, while I get your breakfast.' She must have been as hard as nails, but she was just 'My Mum.'

In my lifetime, I have met some wonderful people, my family; my wonderful wife who put up with me for sixty-eight years. These days I devote my life helping friends and neighbours in any way I can, and I must say they keep me busy and I wouldn't want it any other way. I love it.

CHAPTER 1
Joining Up

It was all Eddie's fault really. There I was minding my own business in Grays High Street on a Saturday afternoon in October 1940 and everyone was still enthusing about the way the RAF had blasted the pants off the Luftwaffe, and for a change people were walking about with an air of 'well show'em (myself included).

'Hello Ron' it was Eddie Gurnett. He and I had known each other since we were four and half years old and had started school together. 'What are you doing with yourself this afternoon? I told him that I was just mooching about with nothing particular on my plate. I'm just going over to Romford to join the Royal Air Force, he replied. 'What on earth for? I asked 'Surely there is plenty of time for us to think of that sort of thing when we get a little older, after all I am only eighteen and besides what would your mum say, when she finds out? 'She already knows' he said. 'Why don't you come over and join with me? I pondered a little. Me, join the RAF? What would I do in the Royal Air Force? After all, I was nearly sick on the big dipper at the Southend Kursaal a couple of years ago, so the Lord knows what I would do going up in an aeroplane.

I confided my fears to Eddie. 'But you don't have to fly if you join the RAF, there are plenty of jobs you can do on the ground.' 'Such as? I replied. 'Well there are instrument repairers like my brother Arthur and well, all sorts of jobs.'

Before I knew where I was, Eddie had persuaded me to join him on the 'Coffee Pot' the affectionate name given to the local 'pull me-push me two carriage train that ran between Tilbury and Romford. We found the RAF recruiting office at Romford and we walked inside and found a beaming sergeant sitting behind a sad looking desk. 'Come in lads, have a seat.' This was not the terrifying man, sergeants were supposed to be. 'What can I do for you? Eddie spoke up. 'We want to join the RAF.' 'Do you now', he answered. Well, you have come to the right place! He's quick, I thought, we didn't come here to join the Brownies. What do you want to do in the RAF, he asked, we are very short of bomber crews and young lads like yourself would fit the bill nicely. After my stomach had clawed its way back out of my socks, I managed to say weakly, thank you very much, but it was not what I had in mind. 'Well what do you want to do then, lad?' asked the sergeant. I felt like saying that I wanted to go home to Mum, but Eddie was firm, too firm. 'We want to be instrument repairers like my brother Arthur. The sergeant didn't know Eddie's Brother Arthur and what's more didn't wish to know about his brother.

At last a desperate plea. 'Are you sure you didn't want to join aircrew, after all you could be a sergeant like me in a couple of months.' What on earth made him think I wanted to be like him? Instrument repairers' said Eddie. 'Sergeant' said the man behind the desk. 'Call me Sergeant.' He suddenly realised we were still 'orrible' little men still in civvies.

Eddie and I filled in the forms and completed our test papers. I was relieved to find that I could still do my fractions and decimals. The sergeant took our papers and told us to wait. We waited and waited. Then an airman with propellers on the arm of his tunic told us to follow him to another room and told us to wait there. He was so superior I thought he must be at least an Admiral, but that could not be, that I did know.

As we waited, I thought of the time about four years previously, when I together with my cousin Les, had cycled to Hornchurch aerodrome to learn a little about the RAF, in order to get our airman's badge in the Boy Scouts. There, we spent three rather pleasant Saturday afternoons with some very nice bods, who treated us kindly and showed us over some Hawker Hinds and Super Furies.

The door opened and a voice said 'Come in'. We walked into the office, where we met a very pleasant officer with a 'handle bar moustache', who informed us we had both done well and he would be pleased to have us in the Royal Air Force. We would have to be attested and I wondered if that would hurt; but he explained that being attested merely meant that we would be sworn in. At that, we were shown out and for the first time I began to think, I was an airman.

Eddie and I were thrilled at the thought of being accepted into the RAF and travelling back to Grays on the old 'Coffee Pot' we were so excited. This excitement lasted until I got back home, when I had to tell my parents what I had done. Then I got cold feet. Mum hit the roof, when I finally plucked up the courage to tell them, but Dad took it rather well, saying something to the effect that he would rather see me in the RAF, than being in the PBI (Poor bloody infantry). My young sister who was ten years old at the time, demanded to know what the PBI meant, but for some reason, no one elected to tell her.

Came the time for our attestation, Eddie and I had to travel up to Cardington in Bedfordshire on 21st December, where this would take place in an old airship hangar. I remember how astonished I was when I saw the size of the place; it was enormous and one could only stand and wonder how big the old airships really were. Anyway, we took the oath and took the King's Shilling and then made our way home to our families, to be with them for Christmas.

I remember celebrating our acceptance into the RAF, by having a drink with our friends at the ARP Headquarters at Grays, where Eddie and I had both been attached since the Munich Crisis in 1938. Major Hampson told us he was proud of us, but he would sooner see us in khaki, but all the same, he and all our friends at Farley House, wished us the best of luck. All we had to do now was wait.

I was on my way home from work, when Dolly dashed out of the butchers shop to tell me rather breathlessly that my calling up papers were at home. She said that my Mother had been into the shop that morning and had told her. Would I write to her when I joined up? We had been friendly since school, and I said that I would.

Mum was red eyed when I walked indoors and for the first time I felt I had done wrong in volunteering and not waiting to be called up. My elder brother told me he thought I had done the right thing, and wished he could do the same thing, but as an electrical engineer, he was in a reserved occupation and his firm prevented him from joining the armed services.

February 5th 1941 dawned, and it was raining. My case was packed and I was impatient to go. I felt fine until it was time to say good-bye to my sister. She threw her arms around my neck and sobbed her heart out. It was no good, I broke down, although, I had vowed that I was going to be a man when it came to say good-bye. Dad walked to Grays Station with me, I don't know how I felt, we had been very close and we had never had a cross word. We met Eddie and his father at the station, and as the two fathers started to talk about how they joined up in 'their war' I felt that at least when the train pulled out of the station, Dad would not be alone.

We said our good-byes, the train was on time and Eddie and I were on our way. It was funny really, I had never been far away from home, never farther away than Ramsgate and here I was heading for Blackpool, the RAF and heavens knows where after that. I was going to war.

CHAPTER 2
Training & Posting

'You've heard of a seaside place called Blackpool, tis noted for sunshine and fun;
Well Mr and Mrs Ramsbottom went there with young Albert, their
son............

So went Stanley Holloway's famous ditty, but my introduction to
Blackpool was thousands and thousands of men in air force blue. The
very first airmen we saw there were two very large corporals with
white caps. 'You two – over there,' one of them shouted to us, over
here, 'at the double.' We didn't know what he meant by 'at the
double.' I thought perhaps it was one of the quaint expressions used
by the RAF, referring to the two of us, but we walked over to him and
his friend and murmured 'Good Morning' or something like that, and
we were made to know in no uncertain manner that were not to talk
to corporals in a friendly way. Corporals were corporals and we were
'the lowest form of animal life.' We were to fall in with the other
bewildered looking men outside the station, 'And don't forget to say
Corporal.'

We were allotted our billet, and were told to be on parade at 08.00
hours the next morning. This we did, together with the other inmates
of our billet, and we spent the entire morning at the Blackpool Tower
Ballroom parading and lining up for the princely sum of two shillings
– our first pay from H.M. Government. In the afternoon we were
vaccinated, inoculated and given the rest of the day off- to go back to
the billet to recover from out jabs. The next day we were a sad and
sorry bunch of airmen – we couldn't lift our arms to shave, we helped
each other to do our ties up and other little jobs we couldn't manage
ourselves. We managed to get through the day; most of us were
scalped, - pardon, given a 'regulation haircut' given an F.F.I. then
visited the Dentist and stamped A.1.

The third day dawned, and everyone was eager to get on the parade
at this was the day when we were to be issued with our uniforms (Ha
Ha!) You never saw such a bunch of weird looking misfits in your life.
Your tunic was either too large or too small. You either had a size 7 ¼

cap or you went without, so that the cap went down to your ears (thank heaven for your ears) or you went on parade with your own headgear, (If you had any, that is). Sorry, we have no ties left, no size 8 boots, if your trousers are too long; tighten your braces further, what a shower. The first time we went out on parade it was something we thought could never be possible. Men with trilby's, bowlers, cloth caps and size 7 ¼ Forage Caps trying hard to keep them out of their eyes, men with red ties, green ties striped ties, men with suede shoes, brown shoes, boots, trousers halfway up their legs, trousers that were standing 'at ease' when the owner was standing to attention, tunics that were made to fit anyone except you, in fact it seemed as though the R.A.F were hell bent on making you the biggest bunch of misfits ever assembled together.

Then, the first time we had to parade in our so called uniforms was hilarious. Every time one of the squad appeared, we all howled with laughter and took the mickey out of each and every man in the squad. The corporal in charge of our squad almost died of apoplexy when he saw us, this made things worse, for we were in tears laughing at his despair when he tried and pleaded with us to tidy ourselves up.

We hit on this idea of swopping different items of clothing with each other (Your tunic is too small, mine is too large, see if it fits). For a while Blackpool sea front looked like Romford market with all the clobber flying around and when we had finished, we still had men with various coloured ties, suede shoes, bowler hats, etc…still, we were airmen now, and were determined to show it. As we proudly walked the sea front, we saluted Air Force Officers, Naval Officers, Army Officers, Bus Inspectors, Gasmen, Milkmen, and anyone else unfortunate enough to wear a peaked cap.

The stay at Blackpool was short, and we were deported to Wilmslow for drilling. The camp was miserable, for it rained most of the time we were there, and our life was one round of marching, counter-marching, rifle drill and more marching. We were dumped on one Corporal Johnson, who, we were to find out, was the most patient man you could ever wish to meet. He nursed us with our marching, our rifle drill and our P.T. We noticed that while other corporals screamed, tore their hair and gnashed their teeth at their respective squads, Corporal Johnson would say 'Come on you numbskulls, you can do better than that, 21 Squad is going to be the best squad on the camp'. With this encouragement we did our best to be the best squad around.

Again, our stay at Wilmslow was a short one. Again, we were deported, this time to Skegness. We hoped fervently that someone would love us and not keep showing us the back door. Our billet this time was very nice. It was just off the sea-front, and before requisitioning must have been a high class hotel.

We were very happy here, and Corporal Johnson's numbskulls made rapid progress to becoming 'real' airmen. We marched in step, without tripping base over apex or stamping on the man's toes behind you. We could also give a smart 'eyes right' without everyone's cap falling off and being trampled on by the rest of the squad. This, I think, was our proudest achievement.

Passing out was achieved without incident. Corporal Johnson told us (as he must have told every other of his squads) that we were the best bunch of 'bloody numbskulls' he had ever had. I don't know whether we really believed him, but all the same we all chipped in and bought him a Ronson lighter inscribed 'from the bloody numbskulls'...'And so we say farewell to this pleasant land' – so went the famous American travel commentary, and as all good things have to come to an end, we had to entrain once more, this time to Melksham in Wiltshire. Here, we were to be trained as Instrument Repairers (or 'bashers') as we were to be known in the 'mob'.

We were informed when we arrived that a two-year course was being condensed into a 13-week course, and we were expected to act like men and absorb this course without problem. Naturally, we did our best, and spent most of the evenings swotting and testing each other, to find out how much we had really learned. The concentration of knowledge crammed into us took its toll however, and three men from out intake had mental break-downs. 'They're coming to take me away; away they're coming to take me away.'

We did however manage to take in some of the surrounding towns, and we visited Trowbridge and Chippenham. It is worth mentioning here that I and another airman 'hitchhiked' from Chippenham, and we proudly arrived back at Melksham hanging on the back of a fire engine. Two other 'erks' came back one evening and claimed they have been given a lift back by Queen-Mary the Queen Mother.

Just before the course ended we were told that the R.A.F was desperately short of Group 1 Instrument Fitters and we were asked to make a special effort to make the Group 1 status and return to Melksham for a further course.

This didn't appeal to many of us, but the extra money was dangled before us like a carrot and spurred on many married men. When the results were published, Eddie had qualified for the Group 1 course, but I had only passed the Group 2 course and would be posted accordingly. On reflection, I was relieved, as I felt that I had had enough of school for a while, but at the same time Eddie and I would go our separate ways after 15 years of friendship. We had started school together, joined the Boy Scouts, started our careers with the same company at the same time, joined the A.R.P. together, and finally had spent 8 months in the RAF together.

A few days before we went on leave, our postings were announced. I was posted to No. 91 Squadron at Hawkinge in Kent. This was a name I would remember, and a name any 'erk' who had been stationed there would remember with pride, although at the time of my posting, I had never heard of it, and hadn't a clue where it was. My immediate concern was my pending leave, and wondering how I would spend 14 whole days at home. I didn't know that after my leave had ended, I would be dramatically introduced to warfare by the opposing air forces, but I was.

I found out that Hawkinge was roughly 70-miles from Grays, so it would not take that long to get there. What I didn't know was that I would have to travel to Tilbury by train, cross the Thames by ferry boat, then take the train from Gravesend to Strood and change to get to Maidstone Barracks, change again to go to Ashford and then to

Folkestone before catching the bus to Hawkinge. Five trains, a ferry and a bus to do 70-miles, I ask you!

Hawkinge aerodrome lay on the cliff tops behind Folkestone and the first time I saw it was when the bus, that had brought me from Folkestone, chugged its way towards Swingfield. It seemed so sleepy, it was a hot summer day and the air itself was heavy. I stood beside the road watching the bus disappear into the distance, heaved my kit-bag on to my shoulder and began to walk towards the main gate. I was stopped by the Special Policeman on duty and he directed me to the Orderly Room, after examining my papers. At the Orderly Room a general duties clerk told me that they had been waiting for a 'Basher' for weeks and that I would be welcomed with open arms. 'One word of warning mate' he said, 'Keep your eyes peeled and your battle bowler handy.'

I was directed to A Flight and was told to ask for 'Chiefy' Honor. I was taken aback, for at training school a flight sergeant was indeed a very important man, and even corporals blanched and jumped, when the flight sergeant appeared.

Halfway around the perimeter track, I heard aircraft and turned to see two Spitfires coming hell for leather across the field. I stopped and admired the daring pilots for flying so low, but then the 'Spitfires' opened up with cannon and machine guns. At the same time the anti-aircraft batteries opened up, the Bofors guns behind me thump, thump, thumped their shells over my head, and I must confess that I had never been so scared in my life. Ten seconds later, it was all over. Looking around, things were going on as if nothing had happened.

A Jeep pulled up beside me and a young pilot officer grinned as if it was all a big joke. 'Going to 'A' Flight? He asked. I saluted and said 'Yes Sir.' I have just been posted and have to report to Flight Sergeant Honor. 'Chiefy' will be pleased to see you' he said, 'he is short of crews. What are you anyway, rigger or fitter? Neither Sir, I'm an instrument repairer.' He looked at me in disbelief. 'We haven't had one for months.' I put my kit-bag in the back of the jeep and climbed in beside the officer. It was then that I noticed that he had no hat, a silk scarf round his neck, open neck shirt and a scruffy pair of flying boots. This was not like the officers we had met at training school. They were immaculate in dress and manner and did not mix with the 'erks.' This chap was chatty and did not seem to care that I was 'less than the dirt beneath his chariot wheels.' This was a term directed at us recruits by a warrant officer at Skegness.

The jeep pulled up beside two Nissen huts. The officer pointed at one and said 'You will find 'Chiefy' Honor in there.' I got out of the jeep and saluted; the officer grinned and drove away. As I walked in 'Chiefy' Honor greeted me with something like' Glad to see you son, we could do with you.' He then introduced me to Sergeant Hooper and Corporal Goodson. The latter said 'I'm Johnny.'

I was taken to the crew-room where I met the A Flight ground crews. I felt more at home inside two minutes than I had done in my previous six months. 'Did you like the reception Jerry laid on for you,' and are your pants still clean? I know one thing, I thought, I am going to brush up my aircraft recognition. I thought I was pretty good, but to mistake a couple of Me109s for Spitfires was a mistake that could be fatal, and I made a mental note that in future I was going to take it for granted that until I was absolutely sure, all aircraft were hostile.

I soon settled down to squadron life, and although I had never worked so hard in my life, I was happy. The summer of 1941 seemed to go on for ever and the weather was glorious. The only snag with the good weather was that we were constantly operational.

No. 91 Squadron was acting as 'Jim Crow' reconnaissance for Fighter Command, so it was essential that we kept an eye on what was going on over the other side of the Channel at all times.

We were up in the mornings at roughly 3.30 am to prepare the first aircraft for Dawn patrol, and we (the squadron) were two up and two down continually all day, every day. Dusk patrol could be as late as 9.00 pm and we had to wait for their return, so they could be serviced before 'covering up' for the night, so usually our day finished at 11.00 pm.

A few weeks of this soon began to tell, everyone was dead tired with constantly working 18-hours every day, and although there was generally someone on leave, his duties had to be shared by the crews still on duty; so short were we on ground crews. Strangely enough, no one seemed to complain about the continual long hours we worked. For a while it seemed strange to me that a squadron of Spitfires seldom seemed drawn into combat, but with a particular task to perform, our pilots were briefed to observe and photograph any unusual activities that were taking place over the Channel. It was more important to bring back information for the intelligence boys, than to be tempted to 'have a go' at the enemy, and perhaps be shot down with vital evidence recorded on the cine cameras.

Our squadron also acted as escort to the Air Sea Rescue Squadron who was also based at the aerodrome. They never lost an aircraft, the whole time I was at Hawkinge. Our pilots must have found it a bit of a bind stooging around a 'Walrus' rescue aircraft at about 90 mph, when their own 'Spits' could do 300 mph. Again, it was a job to do and other pilots of the RAF owed their lives to the ASR and 91 Squadron for giving necessary cover.

One pilot from Fighter Command owed his life to the persistence of Pilot Officer 'Scotty' Downer, a Canadian pilot from 91 Squadron. Downer was escorting a rescue launch from Ramsgate. The launch had picked up a downed pilot from the Channel and as the launch turned for home, thinking its mission was complete, was diverted by Downer who had spotted a second dinghy in the 'drink.' He dived across the bows of the rescue launch and waggled his wings in an attempt to make the vessel turn around, but the crew mistook his meaning and thought he was merely saluting a job well done. After his action had brought no response, he dived down several times, but as a last resort, he dived down across their bows this time firing his guns. This did the trick. The launch turned and Downer guided them to a dinghy and the pilot was rescued successfully. The national press made much of Pilot Officer Downer's initiative.

He was known as the hero of the hour, but it was a short lived one. A few days later he was married to a local girl and we were all happy for him. We kidded him that this was his reward. Shortly afterwards, he went on a routine 'Jim Crow' and never returned. We were stunned for he was one of those men who we took for granted would always come back.

The 'Jim Crow' Squadron was regularly mentioned in the national press and one paper actually reproduced our unofficial emblem of a Crow in a top hat and waistcoat, bow tie, complete with rolled umbrella under its wing. Just how much it captured the imagination of some of the population was reflected in one incident during a spell of leave. I was walking through Grays (in uniform) so I had to have my gas mask with my 'Battle bowler' slung over it. A young boy spotted the emblem painted on the side of the helmet and shouted for everyone to hear, 'Mum, Mum, look, that airman belongs to that famous squadron.' I could not have felt prouder, if I were being decorated at the Palace, Buckingham Palace that is, not East Ham.

Hawkinge was always in the thick of things. We had been bombed regularly, shot up by Jerry when he felt like it. We had even been

20

shelled by the long-range guns at Calais, but as time went on, we were giving more than we received. Newspapers seemed eager to publish tit-bits of information concerning the 'Jim Crow' Squadron, but for security reasons the squadron number was never given, although I daresay that the Germans knew anyway.

Fame followed popularity. There was 'Moses' (Appendix D) perhaps the most aggressive and fanatical pilot the squadron or perhaps in all of Fighter Command ever had?

'Moses' was a Free French pilot, who at the fall of France had been an interpreter for No. 1 Squadron (Hurricanes). He had been ordered to report to a depot in Nantes, but he had an idea, this was to prevent him from evacuating with the British forces. He could not get aboard any of the several aircraft that were evacuating crew back to England. He eventually found a Bristol Bombay transport aircraft with a broken tail-wheel that the RAF was going to abandon. 'Moses' persuaded some ground staff to start the engines and then flew the aircraft to England with some troops aboard. I wonder if his passengers would have gone if they had known that he was not a qualified pilot.

'Moses' came to us as a pilot officer. He was a small dapper man who kept himself very much to himself. Unlike the other officers on the squadron, he would not associate himself with the 'other ranks' and at times it seemed as though he did not know we were there. He was brusque, and would tell his crew in as few words as possible, if anything was not quite right with his aircraft, and then he would walk off.

We grew accustomed to him and in a lot of ways we respected him. It was not long before he bagged his first victim in combat, when we saw him taxi into his bay and that the guns had been fired, but he showed no signs of emotion as he climbed out of his cockpit. We only knew of his success, when fellow pilots told their respective crews. Every time after that when he took off, he went up with the intention of adding to his score and he did that with monotonous regularity. 'Ere, old Moses got another today' was a regular greeting from one erk to another. Such was his attitude that one day he walked out of the pilot's dispersal hut and calmly announced to his fellow pilots that he was going to 'get a Hun.' Half an hour later, he was back in the hut with another scalp under his belt. His promotion was rapid.

He quickly went to flying officer and then to flight lieutenant, shortly afterwards to squadron leader. By the time he was posted to lead his own squadron, when he left us he had shot down fifteen enemy aircraft. I would like to add an unusual postscript to this. About eighteen months later, when I was stationed at Lympne, there was a massive 'sweep' taking place by Fighter Command. Suddenly an ancient Spitfire MkII landed and taxied to our dispersal. The cockpit opened and out jumped a group captain. It was 'Moses'. 'Chiefy' he yelled, 'I want an aircraft and I want it quickly.' Before anyone could do anything about it, he was strapped in another aircraft and shot off to join the others in the sweep. He explained later that his superiors would not let him go on the sweep, that he had pinched an old Spitfire to get him to his old squadron and then pinched one of ours to see if he could add to his score. He returned our aircraft after the sweep, jumped back into his old Spit MkII and returned to his base as a happy sand boy.

'Moses' was not the only character on 91 Squadron, not by any means. For instance, we had a South African flight commander named Le Roux. He was another man whose aim in life seemed to be to beat the Germans single-handed. He once shot down two Messerschmitt 109s within 30-seconds and then radioed base for further instructions. The controller called back, 'come back laddie and by me a pint.' The national press again made a big thing out of this. A week later, Flight Lieutenant Le Roux was in the news again for single handed, he 'beat up' German fighters on a French airfield and left many damaged and burning.

Perhaps the craziest thing he ever did however, was when he was about to go on leave. He was having tea with his wife on the camp, when suddenly the squadron was scrambled. He left his wife to finish her tea alone; he then took off after the rest of 'A' Flight. On returning, he nonchantly told us he had shot down two Focke Wulf 190s and then rejoined his wife at tea.

Another and perhaps the most famous pilot of the squadron was Ray Harries. He joined us as a flight lieutenant and quickly made his mark by shooting German aircraft down all over the place. Again promotion was linked with success and he was given his own squadron and was posted away from us. Making his farewell speech, he told us 'If any of you lads are ever posted to my squadron, make yourself known to me and say that you were with 91 Squadron at Hawkinge and I'll buy you a pint.' Ray Harries was as good as his word, for some time later when I was with No. 121 Wing (which I will tell you about later) I was at Westhampnett, a satellite airfield for Tangmere and we had a pretty good dance band. Although Tangmere had its own band, we were asked to play at the Officers' Mess dance. We were of course delighted and went by lorry to Tangmere, where we were shown to the Mess.

After we had 'tuned up' and ready to make a start, we were then asked if we would like a drink before the dance started. What a stupid thing to say to us. Did he think we would say 'no thank you?' We made our way to the bar, fighting our way to the front through a mass of officers. It was then that I spotted a familiar figure. I approached him and enquired 'Squadron Leader Harries?' He said he was, and I said to him 'I was on the ground crew with you when you were with 91 Squadron at Hawkinge.'

True to his word, he bought me a pint just as he said he would. Fate is a strange thing, for shortly afterwards he was promoted to the rank of wing commander, the icing on the cake being that apart from his promotion, he was once again given a different squadron, No. 91 would you believe!

After settling down to squadron life, 'Chiefy' informed me that I would now have to take my turn on Duty Crew. I must have looked a bit puzzled for he went on 'as we are the nearest aerodrome to France, we have to go on dawn patrol. This means that we have to have crews to uncover the aircraft and service them ready for take-off at the crack of dawn.' Dawn at that time of the year, August, was about 4 am, so that meant that we would have to be up and about 3.00 am. The aircraft earmarked for dawn patrol would have to be serviced and checked by fitters, riggers, electricians, wireless mechanics armourers and instrument 'bashers.' The engines started and warmed up and petrol tanks topped up before the bleary eyed pilots arrived to sign the '700' form before taking off.

Dawn patrol would involve checking the French coast anywhere and everywhere from Dunkirk to Brest. This could take anywhere up to perhaps an hour and while they were away, us 'erks' on the duty crew would be servicing the next machines, who would be taking over after the dawn patrol came home. This would continue until a truck arrived from Reindene Woods, where we were billeted, to take over from us. Billeting us in the woods was some bright sparks idea assuming the Germans would not see where the ground-staff were, so we would be safe from attack. The joke was, our own pilots told us that our huts stood out like a sore thumb among the trees and some said they even looked for the huts to use as landmarks!

Apart from duty crew, we also got lumbered with aircraft guard. What a hoot! As I have already mentioned Hawkinge was situated just behind the top of Folkestone cliffs, and if we strolled along the lane behind the crew room, we could look across the English Channel and see the French coast, which I assumed was Cap Gris-Nez. That shows how near we were to Jerry.

So there I was on aircraft guard at night, all own my 'Todd' only 20-miles from the Germans, who could almost swim across and I armed to the teeth, well not quite, for I was armed with a pick handle with a spike stuck in the end. I don't know if it was supposed to frighten Jerry, but it frightened the hell out of me, the thought of being confronted by perhaps a hoard of German commandos with machine guns and saying in a squeaky voice, 'Halt' or I will throw my pick axe handle at you!

I know Winston Churchill once said in his famous speech, that we would fight them in the hills and on the beaches, but never did he once mention that we would do it with pick handles with a spike on the end. I know I thought 'you're having a laugh mate,' we would have more chance with a ruddy catapult.

I did have a hell of a fright one night whilst on guard. I was patrolling the dispersal and went to duck under a Spitfire mainplane. As I did, so I felt someone or something grab the collar of my tunic. I was petrified and waited for 'my end.' But nothing happened. Gingerly I felt my collar and found I had caught it on the Pitot Head, an L-shaped tube under the wing, which, when the aircraft was in flight measured the airspeed. That was a terrifying experience and I vowed never to duck under the mainplane again

Life was never tedious with 91 Squadron, nothing was ever 'routine' and there was always something to learn, giving a hand to the riggers, fitters and armourers, but somehow I never got to help the electricians or wireless mechanics, they were too complicated for me. My motto was 'if you can't wind it up, I don't want to know.' That is why I liked to help 'Whacker' Kirk, the bowser driver, for I could start the tractor and get the bowser pump going. This I found rather handy while we were at Lympne as there was no R & R Flight there and there were occasions when the RAF were on sweeps and we acted as R & R.

It was on one of these occasions that I was involved in a once in a lifetime incident. The Germans had recently appointed Field Marshal Kesselring as something like commander in chief of the Luftwaffe Fighter Command. When the news reached our commanding officer, Squadron Leader Bobby Oxspring, he got us all together and gave us direct orders to dig slit trenches near to where our aircraft were parked. Apparently he had crossed swords with Kesselring before and was aware that one of his favourite tactics was to 'beat up' our airfields, so if he decided to 'strafe' our airfield, we would have 'foxholes to dive into. Given the fact that Lympne's tiny airstrip had been given the undivided attention of Hitler's bombers on several occasions, the place was literally covered with filled bomb craters, and now with slit trenches all over the place. Lympne was not a nice place for aircraft to land.

This particular day, the RAF had been on one of their regular sweeps, when a Spitfire came in low and was obviously in some sort of trouble. We watched as the flaps came down, the undercart came down and made a near perfect landing, until it encountered one of our filled in craters and stood on its nose and then turned gently on its back. Instantly, hordes of 'erks', about ten, made a bee line for the upturned 'Spit' and manhandled the fuselage up so that a couple of them could get the pilot out. Much to our relief the pilot pulled himself together, said a shaky 'thank you' and as he took off his flying helmet, we could see who it was, none other than Bob Stanford Tuck, one of Fighter Commands top aces. Happily Stanford Tuck survived the war and sometimes I wonder if he ever thought about the day that could have gone disastrously wrong, I know I do and feel chuffed that I helped him.

When the RAF began to dominate the air over the French coast and daylight sweeps were prevalent, Ray Harries was promoted to the rank of wing commander and by some strange act of fate one of the squadrons under his Wing was 91 (Nigeria) Squadron. How efficient 91 Squadron had become can be assessed by a newspaper article which said:

Individual fighter honours went to a Spitfire Wing commanded by Wing Commander R.H. Harries DFC and two Bars. This Wing destroyed twenty-seven enemy aircraft. Eighteen were shot down by the Nigeria Squadron of which Harries was formerly commanding officer. The wing commander himself claimed three victims.

Ray Harries was one of the most decorated officers in the RAF. The last contact I had was when I was with my Typhoon Wing. He was then a wing commander with Distinguished Service Order and bar, Distinguished Flying Cross and bar, French Croix de Guerre and the Belgian Croix de Guerre with Palm. This was when he bought me a pint.

After roughly one year with 91 Squadron, I began to think to myself as part of the fixtures and it did occur to me that it wouldn't be bad to spend the rest of the war at Hawkinge. Then one day, we were told to pack. The entire squadron was on the move, where to? No one seemed to know. Manston, Tangmere, Detling, Hornchurch maybe, we guessed it would be somewhere within No. 11 Group territory. Anyway, we only went over the hill to Lympne. When I saw it for the first time, my immediate reaction was of disgust. What a miserable scruffy looking place. It looked as though Jerry had just knocked hell out of the place and we had just left it as it had happened. That could not be though, as after a few minutes we could see concrete bases where hangars had once stood. Grass and weeds grew between the cracks of the concrete and as we looked around, it was very obvious that during the past few months, Lympne had had more than its fair share of attention from the Luftwaffe, parts of demolished buildings were evident and filled in craters were dotted all over the airfield itself. Just as we were wondering what sort of place this was, a YMCA tea wagon drove up.

The shutter went up from the side of the wagon and there stood one of the most charming ladies it has ever been my fortune to meet. The way that she spoke and carried herself made it very obvious that she was a well bred woman. Mrs Davis, as we soon found out, had a kind word and smile for everyone, from the scruffiest erk upwards, and whatever the weather or the circumstances, she would turn up with her YMCA wagon to serve us with our 'char and a wad.'

It was Mrs Davis who made life tolerable at Lympne and I doubt if any erk who was with us would ever forget her. She reminded many of us of Mrs Wallace Simpson and one erk remarked one day 'If Mrs Simpson is like Mrs Davis, I can understand 'Teddy' giving up his throne for her.' Such was the regard we erks had for her.

It was about this time that our commanding officer was Bobby Oxspring. We were very proud of our CO, for he was one of the 'Few' and must have been born under a lucky star, for he survived the war and finally retired with the rank of group captain.

CHAPTER 3
Commando - Who Me?

No. 91 Squadron continued its good work at Lympne and by this time we had more ground crews, although from time to time my pals who were 'resident' when I first arrived at Hawkinge were posted overseas. Then the bombshell, 'Binkie' report to the 'Orderly Room.' This shattering announcement destroyed my little world. I didn't want to leave the squadron; I felt I was part of the furniture. Still, I thought it might not be a posting; it may be something entirely different.

At the Orderly Room, my worst fears were realised, I was posted. What does 3203 S.C. mean? I asked the lads in the room. None of them had a clue, but there it was; I had to report to 3203 S.C. at Stapleford Tawney. My hopes soared for Stapleford Tawney was not far from home, just outside Romford, so perhaps I could nip off home now and again. Perhaps being posted would not be so bad after all.

On the train from Folkestone to Charing Cross, I had time to reflect on the time I had spent with No. 91 Squadron. It was twelve months since I had joined the squadron from training school, but it seemed like a lifetime had passed since the day I mistook the 109s for Spitfires. I realised I was going to miss the boys of 91, they were a great bunch. There was 'Tubby' Crockford from Canning Town in London's East End. We were mates from the moment I told him that my mother used to live in Canning Town, when my grandfather was a docker. 'Where abouts in Canning Town' he asked. 'Baron Road' I replied. 'Well I'm buggered, that's just around the corner from me' he said. He asked me if I knew the district very well and I told my knowledge of the area was very scant. A few days later, he said out of the blue, 'what do you fink? When Jerry started the Blitz, we were told to put sticky paper on all the windows, to stop them from shattering.

Well I spent all the bleedin' morning sticking pieces of paper on all the windows and that same afternoon, the Germans hit the docks and blew all the windows out. What a waste of time that was and 'Tubby' was rather indignant about that. The first chance that he and I had to spend a few hours together, he took me down to Folkestone, and after walking round the back streets, he walked into a little pub and said 'Ere we are, just like home.' He walked up to the bar and simply said 'beer, cheeses and pickles for two.' It was just like 'Tubby' said, it was just like any East End pub, homely, no frills, just honest to goodness everyday atmosphere, sparsely furnished, but friendly clientele. I can still taste that meal, today's so called Ploughman's lunch, couldn't begin to compare it. The beer was real beer and the cheese was out of this world. Pickled Onions? You never had onions like them. I don't know why, but going back to camp, 'Tubby' and I had most of the lower deck of the bus to ourselves, other erks and passengers were huddled up in a heap right at the back. Shortly afterwards 'Tubby' was posted overseas and I never saw him again.

Then there was 'Jacko' whose full name I shall hold back, a nice enough chap, but struth, when Eric slept, we had a job too. As soon as his head hit the hay, his teeth would start grinding and when I say grind, I mean grind. He would or could wake everyone in the hut once he started and it would be a right pantomime in the morning; when Jim 'Sunset' Marsden got out of bed. Jim was unfortunate enough to occupy the next bed to 'Jacko' and every morning Jim would get out of bed and take one enormous step, 'to climb over a pile of sawdust' he would explain.

Jim got the nickname of 'Sunset' because he had the ruddiest complexion I or anyone else had ever seen. I once saw 'Baldy' Ward hold a piece of bread on a fork near Jim's face to see if he could toast it. Jim had his own peculiar sense of humour too. If anyone niggled him in anyway, he would out of the blue ask 'do you know Sevenoaks?' The unsuspecting one would say 'Yes' then Jim would say 'then poke five of them up your arse.' When the laughter died down, Jim would then say 'you aren't offended are you? The poor erk would inevitably say 'No' and then Jim would say 'then poke the other two up as well' and stalk off.

'Mac' McCubbine was another character, whose aim in life apart from getting his ticket, was to make a pun out of everything. He loved micky taking, but one day it backfired on him. He contracted some sort of skin complaint and had to have his head shaved. Well, after seeing 'Mac' without his unruly thick hair, we had great satisfaction seeing him trying to keep his FS cap, airmen for the use of, on his head, he was told he was lucky he was issued with a pair of king-size lugholes. He was also offered no end of pieces of string and elastic bands. The funniest was yet to come, 'Pedro' an aircraftsman general duties had spent some time with the International Brigade in Spain, seemed to us to be a wee bit shell-shocked. He would use a dartboard to practice his knife throwing, an art he had picked up in Spain. He would be on dispersal and would suddenly take his boots and socks off and run like the clappers through the grass. Then put his socks and boots back on again as if nothing had happened. Well 'Pedro' decided he would like his head shaved, which he did. The same day, the little station bus which ran us from Reindene Woods, where we were billeted to the dispersal arrived, and we all piled on. 'Mac' sat down in one seat and 'Pedro' sat next to him. They looked at each other, wondering who was taking the 'mick' out of whom.

Bert Trigwell, who lived next door to my mother, was a bus conductor, and he told me the easiest way to get to Stapleford Tawney. I scrounged a ride on Bert's bus the next day and at the depot, he showed me the way to Stapleford. I found the camp alright, but what a funny airfield. There wasn't one. No aircraft, nothing. They had a barrier instead of a main gate. I approached the disinterested looking erk on the gate. 'Where do I report to 3203 S.C' I asked. He looked blank. 'Never heard of it' he said. 'Are you sure you've come to the right station?' 'This is Stapleford Tawney isn't it?' He agreed that it was. He was stationed here and he should know. 'But I still ain't never heard of it'.

He directed me to the Station Headquarters and eventually I found out that 3203 was a new unit being formed and I was the first arrival. Perhaps Warrant Officer Rose knows what we've got to do with this bloke, was one suggestion. As it happened, Warrant Officer Rose was 3203 S.C until I got there. He told me to hang about and keep in touch as airmen from all over 11 Group would join us to form this new unit.

A few days later, we were all assembled in the NAAFI and addressed by the commanding officer, 'You men are creating history in the RAF' he announced. 'Isn't that nice of us,' someone murmured. 'You are the first RAF personnel to belong to Combined Operations; the unit is to be known now as 3203 Servicing Commando'. So that was what S.C meant, Commandos? Us, he's got to be kidding? We looked around at each other, if Jerry could see us and think of us as Commandos, he'd die laughing. Perhaps that was the idea, he'd die of laughing and that would save us the bother of shooting them, very neat.

The commanding officer was serious and continued 'you men are tradesmen, every one of you, but we are going to make you a fighting force so that you may travel with the army, to any part of the world and service aircraft on captured airfields, so giving air cover to the army boys'. That was the idea anyway. We would be given training in unarmed combat, bayonet fighting, we would be at the peak of physical fitness, we would be able to disembark from a troop ship in the dead of night, man landing craft and storm enemy beaches. I say again, that was the idea, but would it work, I thought not, but Tommy Rose and his henchmen had other ideas.

Next day, Reveille and out of our pits into PT gear. Half an hour of physical training; and then a run around the camp about three times. By breakfast, we were all knackered. We just about had enough strength to stagger over to the mess for breakfast. Carrying a knife, fork, spoon, two plates and a mug was just about all we could manage. That was just the start. We had more PT, PT rifle drill and more rifle drill, bayonet drill, cross country runs, unarmed combat until we thought we would drop. Suddenly, we realised that we were fitter than any of us thought we could be. Our reflexes were sharper, we were brighter eyed; in fact, we seemed to be a different bunch of bods than we were a few weeks ago.

One day we were told to pack our kit, we were going on a toughening up course. Toughening up? Someone has got to be joking this time, what did they think we had been doing for the past few weeks? We trained not knowing where we were going, it was May

1942 and I did not know that this was the start of a nomadic life that was to last until July 1945. We travelled all that day and part of the night. The only break we had on that journey was when we stopped at Carlisle and had a cup of the most revolting tea I had ever tasted. We also had a couple of curly sandwiches and back on the train to where? Our journey over, we were paraded and marched to our destination in full marching order. The barrack gates appeared and we were astonished to find ourselves at a naval barracks, which we afterwards learned to be HMS Dundonald, we were at our temporary home at Troon.

The toughening up started easy enough, routine drill, rifle drill, bayonet fighting, unarmed combat etc; but then we started assault courses. This was bad enough when we started but daily the courses were toughened, climbing ropes and scaling walls, crossing imaginary rivers by rope in full marching order was part of the training. One of the biggest jolts I ever had was when we had to scale a 15 foot building, cross the roof and then jump off the other side. Again, this had to be done in full marching order. Although we jumped and landed as instructed, the jolt was terrific. Strangely enough, although some of the naval personnel belonged to Combined Operations, (this was signified by a badge worn by Combined Ops Units), we never saw any of the matelots going 'through the Mill' like we were. Nevertheless, we made good friends with the matelots and we were please that they treated us like a fighting force and there was never a reference to the 'Brylcream Boys.'

We only spent two weeks at HMS Dundonald, then we were on the move once more again, the destination was secret. This was the first time that I had experienced travelling through mountainous country, but the train wound its way through some breathtaking scenery. We still never had a clue as to where we were going; the only thing we knew for sure was that we were heading westwards. Our destination, when we reached it was one that we stared at in disbelief. Our new home was anchored serenely in the middle of Loch Fyne off Inverary, Argyll. We knew then that our CO was correct in everything he said we would do and this was the latest phase in our training. The troop ship looked sombre in her battleship grey guise as she lay at anchor, but we had no idea she was so large until we drew alongside in our landing craft, at least that is what we were told they were. We had to board her by using scrambling nets; that was the first part of our new training schedule. As I scrambled onto her deck, I heard someone say, 'Hello Ron, fancy seeing you here.' The voice belonged to Len Major, my elder brother's best friend. He went on 'they said there were some RAF chaps coming aboard and I wondered if you would be among them.' I thought the statement rather curious, as out of the hundreds of thousands of RAF personnel, he should expect to see me on board that particular ship, it wasn't quite on the cards, but there it was, I did appear nevertheless, we were pleased to see each other.

I cannot say much about the life on board ship, as we weren't on board for very long at one time. It would be 'wakey wakey', down to the mess or whatever you like to call it for breakfast, then parade for the day's torture. This consisted regularly of clambering over the side down the scrambling nets, again in full marching order, hoping that at the bottom was a landing craft. It was a hair-raising experience tentatively putting out a foot when you were at the bottom of the scrambling nets, trying to find your particular landing craft. If there was any sort of a swell, you would put your foot out and the landing craft would mysteriously disappear, then it would come up again and you would fall into it, leaving you wondering how the hell you managed it. We would then 'storm' the beaches and then fight the enemy up the hills and down the hills, and up the hills again for good measure. This was generally done in the ever present 'Scotch mist' and we got soaked daily.

One thing at Inverary, Len told me that he had found something that he had always wanted to find, and that was a pub with a piano that didn't play a single note. He was rather chuffed about that. The climax of our training came when we were woken about 1 a.m. one morning to take part in a landing exercise. We had to dress and don our marching kit without showing a light and by crocodiling up the companionway, we found ourselves on deck. Then it was over the side, down the scrambling nets to the waiting boats below. For a non-swimmer like me, it was one of the most frightening experiences I could ever wish to have. We managed this exercise without mishap and I think we were all pleased with ourselves.

Our training over, we awaited the next move. This wasn't long in coming, for we were told to pack our kit a couple of days later. Again, the train took us through the wonderful Scottish scenery, but this time we eventually headed south. For us southerners it was exciting as we neared London, but for the 'Haggis bashers' and 'Geordies', we had in the unit, it was rather despairing. At last we were steaming through countryside that I knew well and I was rather apprehensive as to our final destination, rather hoping we would stop at one of my old stamping grounds. Sure enough, the train stopped and we were told to fall in on the platform. There were cries of 'Where the hell are we now? 'Westerhanger ? Never heard of it? I was in the position to say with an air of superiority, 'That's Folkestone Racecourse over there, so we are going to Lympne.' We fell in and had to march towards the familiar guard room and as we did so, a couple of Spitfires made a circuit of the airfield, I recognised the squadron markings DL and I exclaimed 'My old squadron are still here.' Yes, I was back to dear old 91 Squadron again.

See, the conquering hero comes, what a welcome I got from my old pals. Pilots and erks alike seemed genuinely pleased to see me, but I got a terrific ribbing about my khaki uniform. Needless to say, all my pals wanted to know what we were doing at Lympne, and when I told them that we were going to service their 'kites', there was a unanimous chorus of 'Your mob ain't touching my kite.' The resentment was because they thought we were the RAF Regiment and didn't know we were all qualified tradesmen. Their attitudes soon changed and we were all soon buddies.

It was great being back on the dispersal, but although we were getting our hand in at servicing aircraft again, we still had to do our regular stints on rifle drill, route marches etc.

We had only been at Lympne a few days, when we were paraded on the square, this was the remains of a blitzed hangar and we were inspected by his Royal Highness the Duke of Kent. We were all very proud, but for me, it was a special privilege, for back in 1941 when I had been on 91 Squadron for about six months, the squadron was honoured by the presence of the Duke of Kent. We were to be inspected by the Duke on the dispersal. I was in the unfortunate position of possessing only one uniform. That was my working and best 'blue', so to keep that tidy, I always worked in overalls. On the day the Duke arrived to inspect us, I was in my overalls which were thick with grease. My superiors decided I was not in a fit state to be seen by the Duke and I was told to sit in the air raid shelter until the inspection was over and the Duke had gone onto B flight. This was perhaps the most humiliating and disappointing experiences of my life, and so to be on parade with 3203 when the Duke inspected the unit, made up for the humiliation I had suffered at Hawkinge.

We had been ay Lympne for only a couple of weeks, when I was given 14-days leave. I went home feeling and looking very fit. This was in contrast to the first leave I had with 91 Squadron, when I went home exhausted after months of working 18 hours daily. On that occasion I got a train from Folkestone to Charing Cross. It was a very hot day and I fell asleep on the train after undoing my tunic and taking off my cap. It seemed like only a matter of minutes later, when I was shaken by a porter, who was saying 'come on son, you're at Charing Cross, you can't go any further.' I must have been in a dead sleep, for I dimly recall taking my bag, gas mask and helmet down from the rack and walking along the platform to the ticket barrier.

At the barrier I was approached by two Special Policemen who asked for my pass and I was told at the same time, that I was to be put on a charge, for being improperly dressed. I must have appeared to them to still be in a slight daze, for apart from still being half asleep, my tie and collar were loose, my tunic was undone with my cap tucked down my trousers and my 'Goon' bag improperly slung. One of the policemen asked me where I was stationed and I told him 'Hawkinge.' The two men exchanged glances and one remarked 'You have had it rough down there, haven't you airman? Apparently, it was well known that we had had more than our fair share of attention from Jerry, for the same chap continued 'We will forget the charge this time, tidy yourself up and be on your way, but don't let us catch you improperly dressed again.' He grinned and turned away. I have never forgotten his act of kindness.

My leave over, I returned to Lympne and reported to the main gate as usual. A shock awaited me however, for the guard, who was a corporal, told me that my unit had moved on. He did not know where, but suggested I might find out from the station headquarters the following day. As luck would have it, they told me that 3203 had moved on to Martlesham Heath in Suffolk, and there was a lorry loaded with stores going to Martlesham that morning, so I could get a lift. I sat in the back of the lorry with the stores, it was a bit of a rough ride, but I got there OK, and re-joined my pals.

CHAPTER 4
Injured & Detached

This was to be the last phase of our training before we went overseas. In addition to our routine drills, we were given instruction on driving 3-ton Bedford trucks. This made a pleasant change and we familiarised ourselves with the local countryside, whilst getting used to driving the vehicles. We had quite a few route marches too, even more than usual, and we took it that this meant we would soon be in the boat. This proved to be true, for we were given jabs for overseas posting and told to hold ourselves in readiness for 'immediate movement.'

At this time, we got a bit edgy, not knowing what was going on. We knew something was in the air, but what? No one knew, not even the Orderly Room 'wallahs,' but there was a mysterious feeling that whatever was going to happen, was going to happen soon. We carried on doing the same thing, route marches, PT, unarmed combat etc; then one day we took part in an 'exercise' with other units to prepare for the 'real thing.' I don't know what really happened, but as we engaged the enemy, I felt a sickening blow on my right knee. As I fell, the thought went through my mind, 'if this was for real, I would probably have been bayoneted.' As it happened, it was not for real and I felt sick with pain. I was helped to my feet, but could not stand on my right leg; eventually I was stretchered off to sick quarters and after examination was taken to Ipswich Hospital, where my knee was X-rayed and my leg put in plaster. I was then told that my kneecap was cracked and the cartilage damaged.

My world was shattered. What was going to happen to me now? Would I be a cripple? I was assured by the hospital staff that I would not be, but my knee would never be the same again. I was taken back to Martlesham and 3203, but all I did was permanent room orderly, then sit on my bed and read. I also spent quite some time in the NAAFI playing the piano. Then came the bombshell. 'Pack your kit lads we are going overseas,' Tommy Rose announced. He then turned to me, 'I'm afraid you won't be coming with us Binkie, not with your game leg. You are being attached to Station Headquarters Martlesham temporarily, then you will be posted, I'm sorry, but there is nothing we can do about it.'

The following day, I went down to the barrack square on my crutches to watch my pals throw their kit on to the waiting lorries; then climb aboard after it. I think I shook hands with nearly everyone on the unit, then the lorries started up, moved off and 3203 was gone. I stood on the square desperately unhappy, alone and slightly bewildered. The lorries had vanished out of sight and I stood not knowing what to do, when suddenly I heard a girl's voice. 'Never mind dear, come and have a cup of tea.'

There stood a WAAF I had never seen before, she must have watched as my pals drove off. 'A nice cup of tea and a chat will do you the world of good,' she went on. 'Come on, I'll give you a hand.' She guided me to the WAAF Cookhouse, which was out of bounds to airmen and she sat me down. 'Usually, only Janker wallahs are allowed round the back of here,' she said. 'I'll let Corp know I have brought you round here, she won't mind.' A couple of minutes later I was having tea and jam tart with the WAAF cooks, all being very sympathetic and rather concerned over my welfare. 'What are you going to do now that your unit has gone? This was something that I did not know. All that I did know was that I was attached to the SHQ. The WAAFs joked that I might be attached to the cookhouse. I told them that I would love to work with them; at least I would have lovely workmates. There was some banter about not much work getting done, if I was attached to them, and after half an hour, I felt much better. The girls had done a good job bless'em.

Soon, my leg was taken out of plaster and put into plaster bandage. I could hobble about now without crutches and before long the medical officer told me I was fit to report for light duties, consequently I was told to report to Corporal Reed at the stores, and would remain there until my next posting came through.

I arrived at the stores and said 'I have to report to Corporal Reed' I told the pretty young WAAF at the stores counter. 'You had better come through here then,' she replied. I was shown to a bunch of WAAFs having their morning break. 'Corporal Reed, this airman says he has to report to you.' I stared, for Joyce Reed was a young attractive blonde with big blue eyes. She was rather aloof. 'Where are you from? My unit has been posted overseas and I am unfit with a game leg,' I replied. One girl spoke up. 'You are the chap who plays the piano in the NAAFI aren't you? I confessed that I was. I also told them that I played the guitar, had played in local dance bands since I was fourteen and had in fact got my guitar in my billet. The girls became interested. 'Perhaps we can have a sing song now and again,' ventured one girl. 'Good idea,' said another. It seemed I was accepted. Corporal Reed had mellowed. 'Seeing as you are going to work with us,' she said, I'm Joyce.' She extended her hand. I took it, 'my friends call me Binkie,' I replied. 'Meet the rest of the girls,' she said, Barbara, Ursula, Connie, Dodd, Joan, Kath and Chris.

I thought my new workmates were great. They were all nice and very friendly too. I was fascinated by the different dialects. Barbara for instance was a local girl and lived at Woodbridge. Hers was the musical Suffolk dialect and I used to pull her leg about being a Swede basher. Joan, too had a country girl accent, but she came from just outside Chelmsford. Chris was a London girl, a bit 'Gor blimey' but full of life and fun. Joyce was also a London girl, but I think she came from the suburbs; hers was not the thick East End brogue that Chris had. Then there was Ursula; the youngest and prettiest girl of the lot. She came from Exmouth and her brogue was entirely different from any other. She was a very quiet and shy girl, and had joined the WAAF because her brother was aircrew and had been shot down.

I loved my few months as a store basher. Most of my time was spent running about in the little 15-Cwt Bedford van, shuttling backwards and forwards from Ipswich to Martlesham and Woodbridge to Martlesham. I also used to help the girls in their various jobs, depending who was very busy and could do with an extra pair of hands.

Then one day, Joyce told me she would like me to take over the boots repairs, uniform cleaning and laundry. I would be working directly with her as this was her particular section. I never realised that so many boots had to be repaired. Although I only took boots to Ipswich once weekly, it seemed as though I was handling them daily. Laundry too, was once weekly, but there were masses of it, the wonder of it was that hardly anything seemed to get lost.

While I was working in stores, I made sure that my kit was kept up to scratch. At clothing parades, I used to help the girls fetch and carry and as a result, any kit that I had that was not up to the mark, the girls willingly changed for me.

One day, the girls had to parade for the Equipment Officer. They were actually paraded in the stores and I had to make myself scarce whilst they were on parade. Soon afterwards I heard the girls chattering excitedly among themselves, and I soon found the reason for the excitement. 'Binkie' said Joyce, 'if you have never kissed a sergeant before, now is your chance.' She and Dodd had both been promoted to the rank of sergeant and Connie had been promoted to corporal. All the other girls had been awarded their 'Props, in other words, had been promoted to Leading Aircraftswomen.

I was very pleased for the girls, but they in turn could not understand why I was still an AC2. I had never had a test since I had left Melksham, and I could not see when I was likely to get on until I got back to a squadron. Until then, I would remain a 'plonk.' Still I was not left out of the celebrations. I went to the local with the girls and we had a great evening.

Shortly afterwards, I was told to report to station headquarters. This was something I had been dreading, for I knew it was my posting come through and I was so happy at Martlesham with my 'girls.' Nevertheless, posted I was, but it was a posting that heartened me. Where was I going? 91 Squadron had pulled me back and I was to rejoin them at Lympne. The girls were sorry to see me go and we had another night out 'for Auld Lang Syne.'

It was a bleak winter's day when I arrived back at Lympne. The clouds hung low and the drizzle that we hated, made things worse than need be. The 'kites' all had their cockpit covers on, which was a sign that the squadron was non-operational.

I reported to 'Chiefy' Honor and he greeted me with something like 'good grief, not you again.' I grinned and told him that that he would have to put up with me, it was not my fault and would rather be with my girls in our cosy stores at Martlesham.

There were quite a few new faces in the crew room and I found out that most of the lads that I knew when I first joined 91 Squadron in 1941; had been posted overseas.

I was pleased to know that we were still billeted at the same place. This was Port Lympne, which we understood was the country seat of Sir Philip Sassoon. We 'erks' were actually billeted over the stables which were quite cosy. This was the first house I had seen which had its own swimming pool, although I never saw it with any water in it. The most any of the 'erks' saw of it was when they were asked to sweep it out.

We spent Christmas 1942 at Lympne, although there was not much to celebrate, but we made the most of it. Mrs Davis made her rounds as usual, bless her heart; she put a wee drop of the hard stuff in our tea. I also had a Christmas card from Joyce Reed and the girls at Martlesham. I was particularly pleased about this, for it made me feel that I wasn't forgotten as soon as I was out of sight.

I wrote to Joyce and told her that I would be going up to Martlesham during my next leave, as I had left my guitar and one or two other bits and pieces in her care, as when I had been posted, I felt that my leg was not strong enough to carry all my kit at once.

With Christmas over, 91 Squadron was on the move again. We just went back over the hill to Hawkinge. As much as I disliked Lympne the first time we were there, I was sorry to leave now. The quarters were comfortable, we had a first rate dining hall, which was another country house, a couple of handy pubs and a fair old NAAFI. Then of course, we had Mrs Davis, who would be missed by all of us.

It was about this time, that one of our Spitfires had been on a 'Jim Crow' and had come beetling back and reported that he had seen German battleships leaving the French port of Brest. The weather had been atrocious and very little activity had taken place at Lympne. The clouds always seemed to hang so low, that it seemed as though no sooner had our 'kites' taken off, they were already in cloud. Anyway, there was 'panic stations' as soon that it was learnt that the German vessels had flown the nest. Aircraft were up and down like Yo-yo's and it was a bitter blow when the German fleet crept through the Channel practically unscathed. Our hearts went out to the Fleet Air Arm boys, who had tried so hard to stop the enemy in their obsolete Swordfish torpedo biplanes.

They must have known when they took off to take on the German fleet, together with the Luftwaffe air cover, that they only had a one-way ticket. Apart from the sorrow that so many gallant men had giving their lives for nothing, there was anger and resentment that men had been thrown into the fray with such ancient aircraft. If we had developed such wonderful aircraft like our Spitfires and Hurricanes and bombers like the Wellington and the up and coming Lancasters and Halifaxes, why hadn't we developed something that the Fleet Air Arm boys could have had some sort of chance?

My leave came around and I spent one day at Martlesham with Joyce and the girls and picked up my guitar to bring home with me. It was nice to see the girls again, which made me wish that I hadn't been posted away. We had a cup of tea in the stores together and then it was goodbye. I hoped that one day we would see each other again, but this was not to be. I left Martlesham that afternoon and never saw any of the girls again.

Back at Hawkinge, life was very much routine. The squadron continued with its 'Jim Crow' duties and we were always at 'Readiness.' This was even more so now because the army had just carried out their disastrous raid at Dieppe. Although everyone was thrilled at the impudence of the raid, we soon realised what a tragic disaster it turned out to be. In my mind's eye, I can still see the banner headlines of the News of the World paper. 'We land again in France,' they shouted at us. Almost everyone believed that this was the much awaited second front, and when we withdrew from Dieppe, we thought that this failure proved that a landing in France would now be out of the question. This train of thought was wrong however, and just two years later I would take part in the invasion of Normandy.

Fighter Command had now by this time assumed the role of the hunter instead of the hunted; numerous sweeps the previous summer had driven the Luftwaffe inland and had therefore spoilt the fighter boy's fun of beating up Jerry's coastal aerodromes. Dear old 91 was still acting as 'Jim Crow' and so any deviation from routine was always very welcome.

One such deviation happened when our truck arrived at dispersal one morning, as we jumped from the back of the vehicle, we rubbed our eyes in disbelief, for there parked nonchantly among our Spitfire Vs was one slightly damaged 'Wimpey' or to the uneducated, one Wellington bomber. She had a few shrapnel holes in her fuselage fabric, but other than that she seemed perfectly airworthy.

Our immediate concern was for her crew, but we need not have worried. It appeared that the 'Wimpey' had got slightly lost on the way home from an operation and had subsequently run short of fuel. The crew decided to lob down at Hawkinge, but had they known Hawkinge, I think they would have changed their minds. Anyone knowing this dear little drome would say immediately that it was small even by 'Fighter' drome standards.

How the heck the pilot had got it down, we still don't know. It must have been a masterpiece of flying. Either that or his petrol tanks must have dried up right at the last moment. Anyway the R&R boys tanked her up, and the crew turned up laughing their silly heads off, and after a bit of banter on either side, decided they would go home. Off she taxied across our uneven grass, right over B Flights corner and literally turned around on the perimeter track. She sat there for a while, we could not make out whether she was flexing her muscles or whether the skipper was saying to himself, 'Christ, it is smaller than I thought, can I ever get her up.'

Anyway, she shifted her nose slightly, pointed herself straight at us and opened up her throttles. As soon as she began to move, we discreetly moved sharply to one side. Not that we were frightened, we just didn't fancy a short back and sides from her Rotols. As she charged across our little drome, we all willed her to lift. 'Get up girl' came from all of us, but she didn't lift, but still charged straight at us.

As we scattered in all directions, the old girl decided she had had her fun and got herself airborne. We all stood and cheered and waved as she gained height, but almost at once our cheers turned to howls of laughter.

Hawkinge is a very compact airfield and immediately behind our dispersal ran a narrow lane. Right on the edge of the lane stood a small bungalow, which the RAF had requisitioned as an aircrew room and stores combined. The bungalow was tenanted by one LAC Beck (Honest John) to us. John was not allowed to leave the bungalow, as he was responsible for the 'Scramble' phone. Well, as we (pilots and erks alike were watching the 'Wimpey' take off), Honest John stood by his phone. The aircraft got her-self airborne and just cleared the bungalow. The door opened and out came John looking like something from 'Uncle Tom's Cabin.'

We realised what had happened; as the Wimpey just cleared the bungalow, the draught combined with the vibration shook and blew the soot down John's chimney and literally covered him. We were in hysterics to see John's black face with two little white eyes. Things became even more hilarious, when John saw the funny side of things, dropped to one knee, flung his arms wide open and said simply 'Mammy,' impersonating the singer Al Jolson.

CHAPTER 5
2nd T.A.F Hitler's Days are Numbered

It was about this time that postings seemed to drop off considerably. No doubt the way things were going in North Africa had something to do with this, although now and again some poor 'erk' was posted 'on the boat' presumably to the Far East.

We were in good spirits really, Monty's 8th Army was giving Rommel a pasting in the Western Desert, the 1st Army had landed in Algiers and for the first time since I had joined the 'mob' it looked like we could really win the war.

Then it happened. I was ordered to report to the Orderly Room. My fears were realised, but not in the way I thought. I was told that I was on a two-week detachment and to pack only my light kit. 'You are to report to 121 Wing at Wrexham by midnight on Sunday,' I was told. As it was Friday, my immediate thoughts were at least I could get a crafty week-end at home. The Orderly Room 'wallah' fixed me up with my warrant etc and informed me that the 14.30 from Paddington would get me to Wrexham in plenty of time. I caught the first available bus to Folkestone. There I had the luxury of getting a train straight through to Charing Cross. I then travelled by District Line to Tower Hill (or Mark Lane as it was known then). A brisk walk round to Fenchurch Street and then train straight to Grays.

The weekend went very quickly and in no time at all, I was back on Grays Station platform waiting to go to Wrexham. I arrived at Paddington, but which platform did the 14.30 to Wrexham go from? Porters and station masters all shook their heads. 'No such train,' 'but our chap said there was,' I replied. 'We say there ain't no such train, and it's our railway, so we should know.

I asked where the railway ticket office was and was shown, and off I went knowing darned well, they would never believe my story. As I walked inside, there was George Stubbs from B Flight, all hot under the collar. 'Well that's what they told me, and I got here in time to catch it, now they tell me there is no such train.' I prodded George and said 'don't tell me you are after the 14.30 to Wrexham too. 'Thank gawd someone else was told the same thing,' said George. The railway chap shrugged his shoulders and said something to the effect that our Orderly Room had dropped a clanger, he gave us a chit of some sort and informed us that the first train was at 19.30 hours, and be sure to be on it.

'Crikey, five hours to wait! What were we going to do? George came up with the answer. 'I'm going home,' he said. 'It won't take long to get to East Ham.' He looked at me and said 'Come on. You can have a bit of tea with us at home; I can't leave you here on your todd all this time.'

Good old Georgie, a typical East Ender, hard as nails, but soft as you know what. We spent a couple of hours at his home and after my thanks and good-byes, we were back at Paddington and on the night train bound for Wrexham.

God knows how long the journey took that night, but I remember it was daylight when at long last we reached Wrexham. Streuth. What a place. Heavy grey clouds, a biting wind and about six inches of snow on the ground, what a welcome.

George and I made our way to the railway ticket office and asked the way to the aerodrome. 'What drome? We don't know of any drome.' 'Oh no, not again,' we thought. 'But we are posted here,' we protested. 'There must be a drome. How can we be posted to 121 Wing, if there isn't any drome? After some hurried consultations they decided that it must be the new place up the road, so on the back of a 15-Cwt Bedford, we went up the road. We stopped. 'Is this 121 Wing,' we heard the driver ask. 'Yes, this is it,' we heard the reply, so George and I jumped off the back of the lorry with our kit.

There was no Guard Room and my thoughts flashed back to when I joined 3203 S.C. 'Here we go again, another unit of sweet Fanny Adams.' At the gate, was a small stout corporal and a rather jovial looking warrant officer. A jovial warrant officer? No, it can't be. But there he stood, decidedly jovial. We came to attention. 'Reporting to 121 Wing, Sir,' I said. 'Let's have your papers then lads,' he said

Had we heard right, lads he called us, not airmen. He laughed; he could see we were suspicious. 'You are the first airmen to arrive apart from Corporal Griffiths and myself to form 121 Wing. I am Warrant

Officer Faulkner.' Warrant Officer Faulkner, Griffiths, Georgie and myself, we were 121 Wing. At that time neither the four of us, and even Adolf Hitler didn't know it, but the days of the Third Reich were numbered. 121 Wing was to become one of the RAFs most efficient fighting machines of the war, and I was to become part of it.

Bods began to roll up in droves, and in a few days the place was seething with bewildered looking 'erks' all wondering what the hell this was all about. We asked corporals, corporals asked the sergeants, the sergeants asked the flight sergeants, but they knew just about as much as we did. Every now and then someone would come tearing into our tent and say, 'heard the gen? Natter, natter, natter, 'I know it's pukka, cos Taffy in the cookhouse told Ginger, and Ginger said the cookhouse always know first.' Sadly, the gen was always duff.

One miserable day, we were sitting in our tent, when we heard it. Or did we, we listened and looked at each other, yes it was, no doubt about it, a girl singing, a real female lady singing in our camp, where there were no females. We all grabbed our caps and dashed off towards the singing. It came from a building that resembled a hangar and we yanked the door open and saw a crowd of 'erks' looking and listening.

Our female was a tall, dark haired 'erk' and although we were all shattered at the let down; we were nevertheless spellbound by the quality of the voice, which was a definite soprano. The voice belonged to George Edwards, who through 121 Wing's subsequent concert party became a great pal of mine.

The very next day, we were parading in the same building and were told officially why 121 Wing was formed. We were the first unit of a new branch of the RAF. We were now part of 2nd Tactical Air Force, and our role was to be the supporting air force to the ground forces, if and when we invaded Europe. The plan was to form mobile units of specially trained men who could lead a nomadic life. The men, who would be servicing aircraft, would be capable at the drop of a hat to pack up his tools, his kit, his portable hangars and load them onto lorries and be ready to move. This applied to everyone, the cooks would have to dismantle their cookhouse, clerks, would dismantle the orderly room and so on. We shook our heads, it would never work, how could it work? We would need electricity, water, tools, sick bay; no it was out of the question. The top brass were asking too much this time. Also we thought. The top brass said it would work, and they meant it to work. So much depended on it? Someone had to service aircraft on emergency airfields in the event of an invasion. If the ground forces had no air cover, then the invasion would be a repeat of Dunkirk or Dieppe. Second Tactical Air Force had to succeed. This was hammered home to us. If we failed, we were finished. Jerry would win the war. It was as simple as that. So we would be a success. Jerry wouldn't win, not if we could help it.

The briefing over, we were given a brief lecture by our newly appointed medical officer, Squadron Leader Davis. His text was simple, if we were to be a successful unit, much would depend on the health of the personnel. Health could depend on hygiene, so be careful. Don't leave scraps of food lying about which could encourage rats, mice, flies. Be particular with the latrines, wash carefully and regularly and be very careful with female acquaintances. 'If she says no, she means maybe. If she says maybe, she means yes, and if she says yes, then for goodness sake leave it alone or you can bet your boots there have been dozens before you'. Venereal disease is a weapon the Germans employ particularly against our seamen in foreign ports and it is not above him to employ these methods elsewhere, so leave it alone. Here ended the first lesson.

Time passed slowly at Wrexham, we waiting until our requisite number of 'bods' had arrived and things started to get organised. I was not particularly happy with the initial arrangements whereas we had a gaggle of East Enders in our tent, George Stubbs, Blondie Beckett, Smokey Box and myself; we had to split up. Fitters would bunk in with Fitters; Riggers with Riggers, Motor Mechs and Drivers would bunk in together etc. Unfortunately, Georgie was an FME, Smokey was an MTM, Blondie was a Despatch Rider and yours truly was a Basher. I found myself with a cosmopolitan bunch in my new tent, Bashers, Electricians and Wireless Mechanics. Rog Rogers was from Wiltshire, Bob Lyons came from Huddersfield, Wilf Fanning was from the Black Country, Jimmy Walker was from Bradford, Stan King was from 'town' and Bill Sale I think was another Tyke.

Lindesey, or to give his full name, Thomas Lyndesey St. Clair Steel, was from Edinburgh.

He was unique as far as we were concerned. He was quietly charming, aloof and very definitely eccentric. He would address us all by our surnames as if addressing peasants on the estate of his ancestral home. We took it all in good part for we knew that he was harmless, it was his way, and we all liked him. We particularly liked to hear him during the evenings, when he would quietly talk to no one in particular, and he would talk as though reading a passage from a 'Jeeves' novel. He would perhaps light a cigarette. In doing so, he would start talking, accompanying himself with the appropriate actions. Lindesey, as suave as ever, uncoiled himself elegantly from the couch, reached inside his silk dressing gown and withdrew his platinum cigarette case, opened it and carefully selected a Balkan Sobranie cigarette and lit it with his gold cigarette lighter, inhaled luxuriously and blew smoke towards the ceiling. I used to like to hear Wilf Fanning (Fanny as he got to be called) when Lindesey had finished. 'Turn it oop fer Chrissake Lyndesey, thars got loose marbles or soomat'.

Eventually, we had to leave Wrexham to start our training in earnest. We packed our kit, and for the first time took down our tent, it was a mess to say the least. It was a technique we learned over the next two years, to whip our tents down as neat as a bed roll waiting for the CO's inspection. We got on board the lorries (what a shambles), kit, tools, tents, that was alright, but we hit one small snag; where were we going to travel? 'In the ruddy back with the rest of the rubbish' that's what we were told. We were then politely informed that had we taken more pains over the packing and loading; then there would have been more room for the personnel. We made a mental note to be good boys and do what the nice Sergeant said 'take more pains over the packing and loading', here ended the second lesson.

Having mastered the art of loading our lorries together with reasonable travel in comfort, we were assessed as being capable of moving 'at the drop of a hat'. In this respect I was rather fortunate, for Allen Hemmings and I were assigned to drive the Power Tender.

Our original PT was an old Fordson which was designed as an ambulance. The chassis was fine, but the extra height of the power unit being fixed on the top of the chassis made it a very 'hairy' vehicle to drive. It would sway like the clappers on a straight road, but cornering over 15 miles per hour made one's hair stand on end, for you always felt the old girl was about to finish up on her side. The only compensation for this was listening to the cries of anguish coming from the back of the PT every time we took a corner.

The Transport Officer partly solved the problem when organising the convoy. He quite rightly maintained that the convoy should be governed by the slowest moving vehicle. This turned out to be the Coles Crane which was driven solely by Jim Whittaker. After the Crane came the Petrol Bowser and then 'wallowing wonder'. At this point I must mention that we had two Despatch Riders.

One was given to a chap who thought riding a motorcycle was far better than sitting in an uncomfortable lorry surrounded by equipment. He dropped a bit of a clanger when he was given his bike, a dirty great Harley Davidson. He was visibly shaken when he first saw it; I suppose he had visions of a nice little Excelsior 125! We felt sorry for him in a way, for it was obvious that he didn't like it, in fact he always looked frightened of it. The other Despatch Rider was a fearsome looking Warrant Officer who looked as though he had just gone 15 rounds with Joe Louie. When he had his cycle glasses on, he gave the impression of a vicious thug. Heaven knows what our liberated friends wondered what they had let themselves in for when they saw him at the front of our convoy.

Eventually, our 'wallowing wonder' was replaced by an Austin PT. Again it was adapted from an ambulance; although we found that it didn't sway as much as the old Fordson and was much better behaved on cornering. The only drawback was that Allen and I missed the terrified howls from the back of the vehicles. Shame!

Came the day when we finished playing at loading the lorries for fun, but for real, whoopee! We had looked forward to this for so long, and now it was really happening. After driving all day, we finally stopped at Cirencester, but only for the night. Up in the morning early and off we went again and eventually we came to our very temporary home with the potty name of Middle Wallop. I ask you, Middle Wallop. You've got to be kidding. I suppose next we will be at a place like Pratts Bottom in Kent or Upper Dicker in Sussex. However, we must make the most of a bad job and do what we were meant to do. We were dumped (sorry, allocated) to a section of the airfield where we could do no mischief and offend no one.

We were paraded next morning and introduced to our commanding officer, Wing Commander Adams. He gave us the good news that we were now on a war footing. 'War footing? What the hell had we been doing since 1939?

There was much muttering among the 'erks', shaking of heads at this novel information. The CO then went on to say that as from now, we would be on field rations. That meant we could no longer go to a nice cookhouse and line up for our breakfast of porridge, followed by something like kidneys on fried bread. No more meat and two veg, with a nice sweet for dinner, and perhaps a nourishing tea with the ever popular cup of cha to wash it down. For the time being at least, it was hard tack and corned beef and beans. Sometimes it was corned beef with biscuits and beans, then beans with corned beef and biscuits. So as not to get monotonous, they would start again etc. The CO then mentioned, or should I say, warned that anyone attempting to cross over to the other side of the airfield to visit the NAAFI would be severely dealt with if apprehended. In other words, God help you if you were daft enough to get caught.

One thing was in our favour though, the nights were very dark and it got dark very early. We were confined to our own little world by a single roll of barbed wire, which stretched the entire length of our confine. Did I mention that some of us had wire cutters or tin snips in our toolboxes? No? It must have been an oversight. Ho hum, who is going to be the first? Get off, no names, no pack drill.

It could be coincidence, but shortly after it got dark, there were empty spaces in the tents. 'I wonder where X is at this time of night. I soon found out, for after a couple of nights our tent flap opened and one of my mates said 'Here you are Binkie, you owe me tuppence halfpenny' and then handed me a nice rock bun and a water bottle full of hot tea. I tell you even a NAAFI rock bun tasted nice then, and I say that with my fingers crossed.

I only ventured out once though. I slipped through the barbed wire and found the runway. Yes, it was that posh, it had a runway. Whatever next? I just started across the aforesaid runway when I heard aircraft engines some way off. I had just about got to the middle when some idiot of a pilot switched on his landing lights. You have heard of rabbits being mesmerised by lights shining at them, well, here was one A.C. Plonk with a pouting ring piece in the same situation. I finally made the other side of the runway just before a dirty great Beaufighter roared past and touched down. I was tempted to go straight back to my tent and risk being called a coward, or carry on to obtain my tea and wad from the NAAFI. I didn't enjoy it much for I had the feeling that all eyes were on me as an interloper. I made my way back, but when I got to the runway, I made sure there were no Beaufighters about. Then I ran like the clappers to the safe haven of my little bell tent. It was then that I resolved never to chance risking my life for the sake of a tea and a wad. Here ended the third lesson.

Westwood Ho! We didn't know it at the time, but we were told to pack up ready to move as soon as possible. This we did for we were freed from the confines of Middle Wallop. Once on the move, we could appreciate the lovely countryside of Wiltshire. After a while we noticed the sun on our left, which indicated we were going westwards. We eventually crossed into Devon, at least I think it was Devon, and arrived at our new abode. Whoever wrote the song 'Where my caravan has rested,' must have had us in mind.

We found out that we were now at Membury. Would we be here long enough to make ourselves feel at home? Not so ruddy likely. After a few days it was 'get packed, ready to move.' This time we found ourselves heading east. Perhaps this time we might, just might, find ourselves somewhere near civilisation. I got to feel uneasy, I don't know why. Oh no! My fears were realised, Middle Wallop! We must have been really naughty boys to deserve a second helping. This time however, we were directed to a different section of the airfield. Not only that, but real aircraft. What are they? Too big to be fighters and not big enough for bombers!

After we had unpacked the lorries and erected our tents, we 'got fell in' and marched off to our dispersal to be introduced to our very own squadron, No. 247. The aircraft themselves were ungainly awkward looking things with an 'undercart' that resembled an all in wrestler with legs akimbo. Not only that, to gain entrance to the cockpit, the pilot had to open a door as if he was getting into a car. It bore the name 'Tornado' and was a direct descendant of the much loved Hawker Hurricane. How this thing came from the same stable, we could not comprehend. Just to rub it in, the personnel not allocated to 247 were to service 182 Squadron with Spitfire MkVbs. How we envied these lucky bods. Beggars can't be choosers however, so we all buckled down and did our best under the circumstances.

I shall never forget the first 'pretend' scramble with the Tornados. The Tannoy announced 'Nos 182 and 247 Squadrons scramble.' Ground crews and pilots alike raced to their own kite and had the pilots strapped in ready for the go. Then it happened or rather it didn't happen. You see, the Tornado was fitted with the new Kauffman starter, which was fired with a cartridge. It was all new to ground crews and aircrew alike, and for something like ten minutes it was more like Guy Fawkes Night.

All we could hear was Bang! Bang! Bang! From the starters, the riggers stood armed with fire extinguishers putting out the fires in the air intakes, when some of the pilots had over-primed their aircraft. Erks not actually involved with the so called scramble, stood around bewildered with open mouth disbelief, astonishment and amusement all rolled into one. Needless to say 182 Squadron Spitfires, which were started with the aid of the jolly old trolley 'Acks' had long gone and disappeared over the horizon, while Fred Karno's lot were still gallantly trying to join in the fray, with not much success.

Casey's Court, which was one of the more polite names given to 247's disposal, survived the ribbing from real squadrons, which was 182s lads idea of a joke. Retribution was at hand however, for shortly afterwards, the Tornados were recalled and in their place came a new variation of the aircraft, this being the now famous Typhoon. Basically, the same aircraft with numerous modifications. Gone was the ridiculous car door, the whole appearance seemed to have been given a complete facelift. We were assured that the trouble experienced with the Kauffman starter had been sorted out. One fitter was heard to say 'yeah, we've heard ducks fart before.'

Suddenly the Ugly Duckling' had become the Swan, not beautiful mind you, but just like its famous forefather, the Hurricane, she was so versatile. Designed to be a destroyer, not a fighter, her four 20mm cannons could destroy anything that flew.   Later on, she was fitted with two 500lb bombs, one under each mainplane and later still two 1000lb bombs. Some of the more popular newspapers called it the 'Bombphoon,' a name that didn't go down very well with us, it sounded cheap and undignified.

In no time at all we took the Typhoon to our hearts, especially when it was recognised by the Germans as the most feared aircraft the Allies had. Suddenly the men we called idiots for designing the Tornado had become heroes, well done Sidney Camm and his team!

It was at this time that Jerry had reduced his bombing raids to 'sneak' raids, this being a pathetic idea of perhaps two ME109s or Focke Wulf 190s to sneak over the south coast, drop two bombs and perhaps a burst of machine gun fire, and then quickly off home again after another 'victorious raid on the English coast.

Enter the Typhoon, the pursuit plane, the destroyer, doing what they were designed for. After two or three sorties when the raiders were destroyed on the way home, Jerry decided it wasn't a very good idea after all.

CHAPTER 6
We all love the 'Tiffie'

'Spring is sprung, the grass is riz, I wonder where the boidies is; the boid is on the wing, isn't absurd, I always thought the wing was on the boid.'

So went one of the ditties recited by erks and WAAFs at this period. It really was spring now, April 1943 and it made us feel good. Isn't it funny though, whenever it seems to be going very well, something always comes along to muck it up? It was no surprise then, when we heard the familiar order to pack things up, ready to move.

Driving along in the convoy, the familiar thoughts arose, wondering where we were off to this time. At least we were heading eastwards once more, so it had to be nearer home. Suddenly out of the blue, we realised where we were, for on our right we could see the majestic Windsor Castle, we had reached Berkshire and still heading east. Excitement mounted when we reached London and surrounding districts along the North Circular Road. Before we knew it, we passed Gants Hill and the odds were on us going to Hornchurch, but no, when we reached the 'Green Man' at Ilford, we turned left. Hornchurch wasn't this way; we should have gone straight on along the Eastern Avenue. We soon reached Barkingside and turned right again, and there we were at Fairlop. Since when was there an airfield at Fairlop? The fairies must have put it there.

It was very pleasant at Fairlop, situated in a populated area, but within spitting distance of Hainault Forest. There was one unusual feature about it and that was the NAFFI was outside the camp and about five minutes walk down the road. I loved to spend evenings at the NAAFI as it had a brand new piano and a jolly nice one at that. I could not make out why so few airmen and WAAFs used the NAAFI, perhaps it was so close to Ilford, where there was plenty of night life, then on the other hand, it was my piano playing that kept them away. The young lady behind the counter refuted the last suggestion, as she told me that she could listen to me all night. I was rather chuffed at that, although I took great pains to style my playing after my favourite bandleader at the time, Carrol Gibbons. It was his simple uncomplicated way, nothing fancy, together with a mixture of 'tenths and back tenths' with his left hand, that made his playing easy to listen to. Right, back to the war!

We were non-operational as far as I can remember, I think it was a change of strategy to get the pilots as many flying hours in as they could, the reasoning I surmise that all pilots were classified as experienced, and not a bunch of 'rookie' pilots. Let's be frank about this, you could not expect to throw a bunch of pilots together with an untried aircraft and call it a 'crack' squadron in five minutes, so that's how it was at Fairlop. Daily inspection was first thing every morning. Fitters, riggers, bashers, sparks and wireless mechanics all made sure that the aircraft were serviceable; then the pilot would sign Form 700. I must add that no aircraft was allowed to fly until the respective ground crew had signed Form 700. This was repeated every time the aircraft flew; as soon as it landed and returned to its dispersal point, the procedure was repeated.

The most horrifying minute of my life happened at Fairlop. It was after one of our 'kites' had just undertaken a 40- hour inspection, and as laid down, the machine had to be 'air tested' before it could be made operational.

On this occasion the pilot, Flying Officer Burton climbed into his kite and took off. As he did so, the YMCA tea wagon arrived at our dispersal. Most of the 'erks' were standing around the van drinking tea and munching away at the inevitable bun, watching Flying Officer Burton putting his aircraft through its paces, climbing, turning, shallow diving, doing all the right things, then he went into a wide spiralling climb, gaining more and more height until it was almost out of sight. What happened next would remain with me for the rest of my life.

Flying Officer Burton turned on his back and put his 'kite' into what we called a 'Stuka' dive, coming down vertically, engine screaming, and we all watched completely transfixed. Then it happened, there was an almighty bang and the complete tail unit parted from the aircrafts fuselage. I heard one solitary 'Oh Christ' No please no! Most of us turned away as it hit the end of the runway, burst into flames and completely disintegrated. No one ran; we were all transfixed watching, I heard the YMCA lady crying hysterically, for she had seen it too.

I don't know if anyone really knew what had happened, the 'Boffins' never knew, they had their theories of course, but nothing concrete. Eventually, all the Typhoons had 'fishplates' riveted to the fuselage. Long after the war had finished and jet aircraft were going through the sound barrier, I happened to hear a plane had gone through a sonic boom and the thought struck me, could it be possible that Flying Officer Burton was the first person ever to fly through the barrier? The possibility is there, for in 1943, no one except a few theorists had ever heard of the sound barrier.

The boffins never really pinpointed the actual cause of Burton's Typhoon, to lose its tail unit. It could be that that I am the only person to come up with this theory. I know that I shall never ever forget that fearsome bang or boom, whatever you like to call it. Aircraft that were shot down, fell down and were never capable of attaining the speed that Burton was doing, he was at full throttle remember, and I doubt if the Stuka hardly got past 300 mph mark, when it reached the bottom of its dive. It was very loud with its siren going, very hideous and unnerving, but quite incapable of getting the speed that Burton's Typhoon was doing on that awful day. I might add that when the Typhoons attacked with cannon, bombs or rockets, it was in a shallow dive.

One other incident that happened at Fairlop was of my own doing. I had been to the NAFFI playing the piano, when I thought I had better make tracks back to my tent. Whilst I was in the NAFFI a thick dense 'pea souper' had descended on the airfield and to be honest I had a job to find the main gate, which in reality was a glorified shed. I exchanged a few words with the SP and carried on. I then did perhaps the most idiotic thing I have ever done. I must explain that Fairlop boasted only one runway. This ran from east to west and was only eighty yards wide. However, to get to the runway you had to cross over roughly fifty yards of grass to reach the Perimeter track, then another fifty odd yards of grass before you actually reached the runway, if you negotiate this, you had to repeat this to get to the other side. Now as my tent was geographically opposite the guard room, it made sense to cross straight over, bearing in mind the Perimeter track was about two miles long. Daft like I opted to cut straight across. Oh what a clanger, I had barely gone about fifty yards in this 'pea souper' when I realised that I hadn't a clue as to what direction I was heading. I stopped, listened, not a sound. All the good airmen were tucked up in their little tents. Which way should I go? Panic began to set in, but I quickly reasoned that I couldn't get lost on an airstrip. About an hour later, I heard voices nearby, I headed towards them as quickly as I could, then I called out. He answered back and I found myself talking to the same SP at the guard room. He made some remark about wandering around in the fog, and I sheepishly started back, but opted for the long way round. If I was perfectly honest, I would say that was one experience I wouldn't like to go through again.

I had a pleasant surprise a few days later though, for I was informed that I was due a week's leave. I dashed off a few lines to my mother saying I would be home on Friday, and posted it off straight away. When I arrived home, I found an empty house, but a note on the table explaining that she, dad and my sister had gone on a week's holiday which had been booked for some time. Apparently Mum wasn't very well and her doctor advised her to have a week by the sea. The letter went on to say that she arranged for me to spend my leave with Mrs Taylor, who was my brother's mother-in-law, who lived at Beeleigh, just outside Maldon in Essex. I knew the Taylor's pretty well; my brother had courted their eldest daughter Vera for some years and eventually married her.

I arrived at Mrs Taylor's house and was greeted as a long lost son. It was made more pleasant than I expected for Vera's younger sister Jean, had grown up into a very attractive girl. She was now seventeen and had altered almost out of recognition, so we got on very well during my stay at Beeleigh. It was very isolated, nothing but very quite countryside, well it would be as it was all farmland. Needless to say Mr Taylor and his son John both worked on farms.

A funny thing happened while I was with the Taylor's, for one morning I was woken by a very worried Mr Taylor, who asked if I was alright. I said something like 'of course I'm alright, why shouldn't I be? According to him, there was a big air-raid during the night, apparently at nearby Chelmsford, where there was a big ball-bearing factory (Hoffmans), but whether Jerry's navigation had not been up to scratch, he had mistakenly dropped his bombs in the Maldon/Beeleigh area.

Mr Taylor explained that they all made a bee-line for the Anderson shelter, tried to awaken me, but had failed to do so and left me tucked up, while they all scuttled to the shelter. I apologised and said that I was so used to air-raids, anti-aircraft gunfire and what have you that; I got to sleep through it all. Mr Taylor scratched his head and muttered something like 'I don't know how the devil you can sleep through a racket like that,' and then went off to work.

The week soon ended and Jean walked down to the Maldon and Heybridge Railway Station, to see me off back to Fairlop. Jean and I wrote to each other for some time, then, she said she had a boyfriend, so that was that.

When I arrived back at the airfield, my pals told me that they had found a way out of the rear of the airfield, crossing a couple of fields to a very nice public house called the 'Dick Turpin.' Needless to say, we spent quite a few evenings down there. The Dick Turpin stood not far from the Eastern Avenue (the A127). It was too good to be true, for I could catch a bus into Romford, from there another bus into Grays. I well remember on one occasion I caught the Romford bus and to my delight the 'Clippie' was Laurie Everett, a girl from the same street where I lived. Somehow, she forgot to take my fare and then told me what time she was making the return journey. Again she forgot to take my fare, kissed me when we reached Romford, then told me to take care of myself. This only happened the one time, for we moved on from Fairlop shortly afterwards.

One night just before we moved on, we were sitting in our tent and it was raining when suddenly the tent flap opened and a strange voice asked 'are you lads all right in there? Before anyone responded, the voice carried on, 'I'm Wing Commander Morice, your new commanding officer and I want to make sure that everyone is alright.'

We thanked him and he vanished into the night. We were astounded that someone would take the trouble to find out if his men were OK, especially a wing commander.

I felt very superior, when I told my mates that Tim Morice was a First World War 'ace' with many victories to his credit. This I did know, for as a boy I was fascinated by the exploits of the Royal Flying Corps. Like any other kid I had my heroes, Mick Mannock, Albert Ball, Billy Bishop, and I also added the name, not so well known of Tim Morice.

As you can guess 'Tim' was knocking on a bit, but he was youthful in his ways and I can honestly say that as far as we were concerned, the finest commanding officer anyone could wish for. Although he was a stickler for discipline, he always had a cheery smile, together with an outstanding memory for names. Happily, he remained our CO for the rest of the war, the last time I saw him was when 121 Wing was disbanded and the personnel repatriated to the UK until demobilisation.

All good things come to an end however, and it was no surprise when we were told that we were on the move again. All the old questions came up again, wondering where it would be and was it a proper airfield or yet another makeshift job. We drove southwards this time, from Essex into Kent, skirting Surrey and finally into Sussex. Eventually, we arrived at Selsey and although it was another temporary 'strip' it was very pleasant.

A change is as good as a rest, so the old saying goes and it was a pleasant change to find that we would be servicing Spitfires, 65 Squadron to be precise. Nothing much happened while was at Selsey, except the one time I ran into Flying Officer Johnny Heap. He recognised me from our 91 Squadron days. He was a good type and like most of our pilots, treated the ground crew more like friends. Having said this, there was always the odd one out, who would come out straight from an OTU, displaying their brand new 'Wings' and treating us like peasants. When this did happen, inevitably one of the more senior pilots would take him to one side and point out that his life could depend on his ground crew, so don't upset them, or you could be sorry.

One funny thing that happened at Selsey was I was awarded a 48-hour pass. I packed my 'goon' bag and toddled off home. I had a nice couple of days at home and then back to Selsey. I got back to the airstrip and there it was – gone. Not a sausage. They had as we use to say, 'been and gone and went.' Where to? I made my way back into town, found the police station and explained my plight. The sergeant was a copper of the old school and he fixed me up with an old lady he knew, so I had a bed for the night and a nice breakfast in the morning. She was a lovely old dear, and refused point blank to accept anything for her trouble. She simply said, she was only too pleased to help one of ours lads in trouble.

Back at the police station, the sergeant told me he was taking me to the railway station, where a 'Redcap' from the RTO would put me right. I didn't like the sound of that, but the 'Redcap' turned out to be a decent sort of chap and he told me where my unit had gone. He could see the funny side of things, adding something like 'they were not very subtle trying to get rid of you that way.' Anyway armed with a railway warrant, I was put on a train to either London Bridge or Victoria, I'm not sure which.

From there I travelled to Ashford in Kent and there to my surprise was a 15-Cwt Bedford truck waiting to take me to Lydd, near Dymchurch. I was greeted with much amusement, some of the 'erks' bowed, curtseyed, and touching forelocks for an erk with his own personal transport. 'Shall I carry your bag Sir? Would you like a single or double room? Were some of the sarcastic digs I had to put up with. 'That didn't work, how do we get rid of you now?' Was also included in the banter.

It was obvious that Lydd was a fairly new airstrip, completely isolated, miles from anywhere and was bleak to put it mildly. The one good thing was that at last we were a Wing, a real Wing with four squadrons, 174, 175, 184 and 247. At the same time and for the first time, each squadron was allocated its own permanent personnel.

I was allocated to No. 247 Squadron as an ancilliary tradesman as we were called, for example, instrument repair, electricians, wireless mechanics and photographic bods, all bunked up together in bell tents. I found myself with 'Rog' Rogers, Stan King, Wilf Fanning, Bill Sayers, Alan Hemmings, Lindesey Steele and Bill 'Leach' Hammond as he liked to be called, they were just to name a few of the bods.

As soon as we settled down and got to know each other a bit better, I was told to report to 174 Squadron, as they had no instrument repair chaps. Strange! They had their own 'Bashers' allocated to them, so where were they? 'Theirs not to reason why?' Was it Lord Tennyson who said that? Mine was not to reason why, just to get over there, pronto. Off I trudged to the other side of the field to 174s dispersal, my little tool case clutched in my hand. It was a good job that the RAF had replaced the damned great wooden toolboxes with the compact little 'Lunch Box' style of toolbox, otherwise I reckon I would have been still walking!

I became a busy little soul, having to look after about twenty-two Hawker Typhoons, but just to rub it in, I also had one forlorn Hurricane as well. I was rather amused at the dear old 'Hurriback' for all the Typhoons had their identification letters, for example XP-A, XP-B and XP-C etc; the Hurricane had the unique marking code of XP-? I had never seen an aircraft before or since, with the identity of a question mark. I don't know why it was there, for it never went on Ops, so I can only assume it was some sort of a Taxi, if you know what I mean.

Life was very humdrum at Lydd, but one thing I did like was at the end of each day, while the sun was setting, one could listen to the 'goodnight' calls of the various species of wildlife, it made you forget there was a war on just for a few minutes.

Another bonus came my way at Lydd, was when all drivers that did not hold a RAF Driving License, would have to have lessons and a subsequent test. A couple of days later, two or three British School of Motoring Driving School cars came on to the airfield and we had lessons on a rota system. Some 'erks' took an early test and passed, leaving us with more time having lessons. I always had the same instructor, he was a very cheerful tubby sort of chap, but he was also very canny. After a couple of lessons he said something to the effect that I didn't need any more lessons, but if I didn't want to take the test yet, it was fine by him; so I had my outings with him, visiting lovely little villages like Appledore, Tenterden and also Rye and Romney. Anyway I didn't want to kill the goose that laid the golden egg, so I thought it was time to take my test. This I did and passed. The examiner said in a suspicious sort of way, that I could have passed some time ago. I wonder why he said that. Don't answer the question.

By this time, a number of personnel had increased. We had our own officer, Flying Officer Pearson, one Sergeant Bob Davis and three Corporals, Eddie Grant, Bob Lyons and Bill Leach. As you might have guessed only one erk; Jimmy Walker. Talk about too many chiefs and not enough Indians - tell me about it.

On the move again, just as we got nice and comfortable, I suppose we shouldn't grumble as this was why our 'Wings' were formed in the first place. As was the norm, we were packed up and ready to move in no time. Someone however, was not satisfied, for we had to unload all the lorries, put up the tents, cookhouse, orderly room etc and erect the portable hangar. 'We do it again tomorrow' we were told and this time do it properly, more efficiently and most of all more quickly.

Came the dawn, after breakfast came the order, pack up, ready to move. Down came the tents; down came the cookhouse and the portable hangar. We done it so many times that it became a mockery. Bye bye Lydd, nice to have met you, where now? Through Kent; up to the smoke (London) and back to dear old Essex, and heading north; on the A12 through Chelmsford, Colchester and bye-passing Ipswich. Soon we were driving through some unbelievable scenery, with tall Pine trees on both sides of the road; it was if we had been transported to Canada. Eventually, someone had spotted Norwich Cathedral, so at least we had some idea where we were going, Attlebridge. Attlebridge? Never heard of it, well you have now.

No sooner had we erected the usual tents cookhouse etc, we began to question, why no aircraft? Something dodgy about this one! We passed the day doing nothing in particular and went to bed. Next morning after breakfast came the order, pack up ready to move.

On the road yet again, this time heading south through Colchester and Chelmsford and heading west. Once through London, we found ourselves on the old A3, which in those days was only a three lane road until we reached Chichester. Were we going back to Selsey or maybe Tangmere? We found our new home shortly afterwards in the shape of Westhampnett, a satellite airfield to Tangmere. We felt pretty much at home at Westhampnett, a nice friendly place within easy reach of Chichester.

This was one of the happiest interludes of late, for one night I wandered over to the NAAFI and a little grey haired airman of fortyish was playing the piano. His style and technique suggested that he was a professional musician and I was dead right.

I introduced myself and he said his name was Cyril Malson, but his friends called him 'Bix.' I thought for a moment; then I said something like 'Bix'? The only other man I had heard of with a nickname was 'Bix' Buiderbeck, an American trumpeter.

He laughed and said that was how he acquired the name, because in reality, he was a professional trumpeter. I told him I was a guitarist and his first reaction was to ask, have you got it with you. I told him it was in my tent, so he asked me to bring it over to the NAAFI. The result was that we had quite a session.

It was not long afterwards, when I went into the NAFFI and I heard the piano being played in a terrific 'Boogie Woogie' style. The chap playing was so good that he was surrounded by a bevy of bods, all watching in admiration. When I was able to get near to him, I told him about 'Bix' and myself, and would he be interested in forming a little 'combo.' He wasn't exactly enthusiastic about the idea, but said he would give it a go. His name was John Todd, soon everybody knew him as 'Toddy.' A Newcastle 'Geordie' through and through, he had a wicked sense of humour. For instance, when 'Bix' asked him if he could read music, he simply said 'it all depends on how many pints I've had!

So now we had a nice little trio, Toddy on piano, Bix on trumpet and myself on guitar. To add to our good luck, we were approached by one of our cooks, Lew Fraser, who told us he had previously played with Lou Prager, a well known dance band leader in London. Had we got a drum kit, he enquired. We all looked in our pockets, but alas no drum kit. Enter our own St. George, George Edwards to be precise. Remember George, the bod with the golden soprano voice, who had fooled us at Wrexham three months earlier. He spoke with words of wisdom. 'I work in the orderly room, so if I approached the adjutant, he may be able to help, as he is also the entertainments officer and has been toying with the idea of forming a concert party.'

It was agreed that George approached the adjutant; he might catch him in a good mood. In the meantime 'Ginger' Woods came on the scene as a quite a pleasant dance band voice, so now we had two vocalists.

Great rejoicing! A lorry arrived with one complete drum kit. Oh happy band of pilgrims or erks if you like. Lew was chuffed at the good fortune and immediately proved he hadn't been shooting a line, when he told us of his capabilities as a drummer. Soon afterwards the adjutant announced that he was going to organise a dance. He was confident that our little band was capable of putting on a good show, so he asked if the WAAFs at Tangmere would like to come along and all ranks could invite their lady friends. As it happened, it was a great success and everyone was hoping that this would be a regular event. The only snag was would we be here long enough to warrant such thinking?

I was given a change of duties while we were at Westhampnett, this being in sole charge of oxygen supplies. Every squadron had large wooden boxes containing six oxygen bottles dotted around their own dispersals. These were for the instrument 'bashers' who had to make sure that all aircraft had sufficient oxygen supplies at all times. If the oxygen gauge read less than three quarters full, then the 'bashers' would change the bottles for full ones, these would be then taken from the wooden box and the empty bottles would be placed in the box upside down, this would indicate to all and sundry, which were full and which were not.

This then, was my task. I was given a 3-ton Bedford truck, which I drove round the dispersals collecting all the empty bottles and replacing them with full ones. Returning to the Oxygen Hut, I then had the job of recharging the bottles, this was done by connecting ten bottles in a rack, which was connected to a master cylinder.

All the valves were then opened and the empty bottles were filled with oxygen. You must appreciate that even master cylinders had to be recharged at times, so when I had sufficient empty cylinders, I would load them on to my truck and drive to Tangmere, where the empty cylinders would be replaced with fully charged ones.

This was no mean feat, for the master cylinders were about twelve feet long and were very heavy, I had to load and unload them on to my lorry on my own. As you may guess it was a very busy job, keeping four squadrons of Hawker Typhoons fully supplied with oxygen, especially when two or three squadrons went on one sortie, all returning together and all wanting oxygen bottles changed at the same time. It was then a mad dash around the airfield collecting all the returned empties and replacing them.

Whilst on this job; something happened that changed my life forever. I received a rather bulky letter from my mother, which enclosed another letter addressed to me at my home address. In her letter, my mother wondered if the other letter was from Winnie. What made mum think this? I had a pretty good idea how she came to this conclusion, but anyway, mum was dead right. I was very pleased to hear from Win, she was a very nice and pretty girl, and we had been out together for a short time before I was called up. We wrote to each other and I took her out when I was on leave. I suppose like a lot of other girls, she wrote and said she was seeing another boy.

Sometime later I read in our local paper my mother had sent, that Win was engaged to this other lad. Anyway, I read Win's letter saying that things hadn't worked out with Denis; she had joined the WAAFs and wondered how I was. She asked if I would write to her. She added that if I didn't want to, she would understand.

Quite frankly, I was overjoyed and wrote back and told her so. I also stated that I would be going on leave on such a date, and could she wangle a leave at the same time. Alas, it didn't work out right then, but while I was on leave I went and saw her parents. Much to my relief, they were pleased to see me and Win's mother went as far to say that she always hoped Win and I would get together again; we had always got on so well. Win's sister Maisie was also pleased to know that I and Win were getting together again. On one previous leave, I had bumped into Maisie and she told me she was getting married on the following Saturday; she said she would love it, if I could attend. Unfortunately, my leave pass was up on the Friday and I was not able to. She expressed her disappointment, and added that if I could have gone, perhaps Win and I could make another start once we saw each other.

I returned to Westhampnett and found they had found a replacement to take over my job of oxygen recharging, so I went back to my squadron, 247. When I reported back to dispersal, I noticed the squadron letters on the fuselage of the 'kites.' This wasn't 247, their markings were ZY and these all had MR painted on them. Then I was informed that 247 had been withdrawn and 245 Squadron had replaced them.

I remember saying to myself 'I wish they would stop mucking us about, we don't know whether we are our apex or elbow,' or words to that effect. Someone up there must have heard me, for I stayed with 245 for the duration of the war.

As 1943 began to draw to a close, the Typhoon was now spoken about on a level as their illustrious sisters, the Spitfire and the Hurricane. It began to show versatility, for now they were fitted with bomb racks carrying a 500lb bomb under each wing. Having said that, the infamous Messerschmitt 109 had already attacked our southern towns, carrying bombs on their 'tip and run' raids. The big difference between the Me109 and the Typhoon was that the Typhoons attacked at squadron or wing strength.

It was not long afterwards that someone at the top of 2nd T.A.F decided that the 'Tiffie' as it was now popularly known, should be carrying a 1,000Ib bomb under each wing. There was much speculation as to whether the aircraft could manage such a burden, after all the old Bristol Blenheim would puff and blow at this bomb load.

I can see us erks and pilots alike, standing watching our first 'Tiffie' at the end of the airstrip, ready to take off with its new bomb load. As it gathered speed, we watched holding our breath and thinking, 'if she doesn't get up, I'm glad that I'm not in its line of take-off.' However, we all gave a sigh of relief when she lifted her nose and slowly, but surely gained height and disappeared over the treetops. A cheer went up, but whether it was in relief or to celebrate the achievement, I don't know.

Soon, all the aircraft were fitted with bomb racks to accommodate the 1000 pounders and the spectacle of watching them take-off with their incredible bomb load was an everyday event.

On the social side of things, we were doing very well. We had the concert party and our fair share of dances. We were asked to play at the officers' dance at Tangmere; the evening went very well and our own officers were well chuffed to think we had gone up in the estimation of the Tangmere mob. I would mention here, that we met a famous character while we were there in the person of Sam Costa; he was a famous vocalist with some of London's best known bands, and eventually became a household name in the BBCs post-war show 'Much binding in the Marsh, with his catch phrase, 'good morning sir, was there something?

It was while serving with 121 Wing that a bumped into another chap who had served with my previous squadron No.91. His name was Johnny Heap, one of our pilots. At this time, we were on exercise at Selsey and had to service a squadron of Spitfires. I was in the process of giving one machine a daily inspection, when I heard a voice enquire 'How long will she be? I looked up and to my astonishment I found it was Johnny Heap. We were pleased to see each other, but it was only a 'hail fellow, well met' as 121 Wing had to leave again after only a few days.

During the winter of 1944, 121 Wing was at an aerodrome in Holland called Volkel, which was near Eindhoven. I happened to be servicing one of the aircraft, when a Hawker Tempest from one of the other Wings sharing our airfield taxied round the perimeter track. As it drew level, it burst a tyre and slewed around; its pilot cut the engine. I jumped down from the Typhoon and jumped up on to the mainplane to help the pilot out of the Tempest. When he took off his helmet, I recognised him immediately; it was Johnny Heap, now a squadron leader. We laughed when we saw each other and I made some crack about him turning up like a bad penny. It was strange running into him again like that, but alas, it was the last time I was to see him.

Shortly afterwards, the Tempest Wing went out on a sweep, and naturally we were all keen to see them come back. As they landed one by one, we watched and counted. In the distance we could see a Tempest coming in low, obviously in difficulties, a trail of white smoke vapour coming from it. 'Blimey, he's hit in the Glycol tank,' someone shouted, 'bale out! We knew he was too low to do that and willed him to make the airfield. It was not to be however, the aircraft exploded and crashed. We were stunned, to think so near and yet so far. I was absolutely devastated when I found out who the pilot was, Johnny Heap. Poor Johnny; who I had known since he was a rooky pilot officer. I kept on saying to myself, 'why didn't you get out when you had the chance? Knowing Johnny however, it was a safe bet that his only concern was to bring his kite back in one piece.

Came the spring, and we were on the move again, this time to Holmsley South, an airfield just outside Bournemouth. This was a very nice place, situated on the edge of the New Forest, with trees on two sides, making it very picturesque.

We hadn't been at Holmsley very long before we were joined by a group of Thunderbolt fighter aircraft from the United States Army Air Force. This was quite a novelty for us, as we had never seen or been near any American aircraft. We had of course seen the Flying Fortresses and Liberators flying out on their bombing missions, but that was as close as we had been. We watched them take-off and return, but the strange thing about them was, they used parachutes to slow them down once they had touched down. We thought it was strange because they weren't all that fast. We came to the conclusion that they were used to runways about five miles long, and didn't like our pokey little airstrips. The other strange thing was we never saw any of their personnel ground crew or aircrew, again we wondered if that was part of their security.

The month of May arrived and all the talk was about the invasion and how long before it happened. Then once again we were told to pack up and get ready to move. This time we headed east and then as the roads turned into country lanes, we headed for Eastchurch on the Isle of Sheppey. After unpacking, we were told the pilots were there for 'air firing.' 'Air firing, you are kidding,' after all we had just left Holmsley South and they had all the English Channel and part of the Atlantic Ocean to practise on, why move about two hundred miles just to pop their guns off, it didn't make sense. 'If ignorance is bliss, its folly to be wise,' so we stopped wondering.

I remember Eastchurch for only two things, both involving our concert party. The first one was when we were rehearsing a sketch, when George Edwards who played the female role in sketches was unable to be present, so the honour this time went to Joe Prior. Joe's line was something like 'hello you gorgeous hunk.' This was directed at Bixie, who was supposed to be the boyfriend. Unfortunately Joe had been to the dentist and had left his dentures there, so when he began to say his lines, poor old Bixie received an unwelcome shower of saliva. Bixie turned around and left the stage, returning almost immediately attired in a black oilskin coat and 'Sou'wester.' He simply said 'right, let's go through that again.' We were in hysterics, all except Joe.

The second incident was when I had to go on detachment to Horsham. I forget why, but it was for only a few days. One afternoon, Flying Officer Willans who was also on detachment came over and said 'Binkie,' we have got to get to Eastchurch pronto! We bundled our kit into his Jeep and set off, thinking it was something to do with the invasion. I asked Willans and he told me that there was to be a concert tonight and that some top brass would be attending, that's why I was going back.

We arrived back at Eastchurch and we drove right up to the hall where the concert was being held. As we climbed out of the vehicle, we could hear George Edwards singing, so we knew the concert was already underway. Having made my way round to the back of the hall, I went backstage and was met by 'Ginger' Woods. 'Oh good, he said 'you are just in time.' He explained that they had slightly altered the routine of George's act, this being when George sang the next song which was 'You made me love you.' I was to wait in the wings and when he reached the line – Give me what I pray for,' I was to walk on to the stage and present George with a candle, bearing in mind that George was dressed in a long flowing evening gown, complete with elbow length gloves and a ladies turban.

Joe Muggins did as he was told and I walked on at the appropriate moment, and as I gave George (who was taken aback apparently ignorant of the change in the act). Anyway the incident had the desired effect and there were howls of laughter. Bixie couldn't play the piano for laughing and I was horrified to see as I turned to face the audience that the first two rows occupied by Queen Alexander's Nurses. The horror quickly turned into relief when I saw the nurses rolling around in fits of laughter. George finished his song to rapturous applause. As for me, I got a dressing down from the Entertainment Officer, who emphasised that in future nothing should be altered without his sanction. Then he grinned and said I could thank my lucky stars that the nurses could see the funny side of things and that no one had been offended. Needless to say, there were no more candle presentations.

Poor George, his life was rotten for the next few days, being subjected to all sorts of cracks about him and his candle. Bix enjoyed it more than most, for he would have a dig and say 'you enjoyed it really, didn't you – you bitch.'

It was only a few days later that we were given the order to pack and get ready to move. By this time, we wondered if nobody wanted us, and the usual questions came up wondering where we would be off to this time. As it turned out, it was a move most of us liked, for it was back to Holmsley South. The Americans were still there, but we had acquired a new recruit in the shape of a Bulldog. He belonged to Pilot Officer Singh, a fearsome looking Sikh. He was a huge man built like a brick wall, but very quiet and aloof. He never had much to say and we didn't know what to make of him, but he was a good pilot and that was all that mattered.

We never had any dances or concerts at Holmsley South, I suppose it was because of the approach of the invasion, but I couldn't help thinking it wouldn't be a bad idea to have a concert, if only to relieve tension that was building up. Then one night, I strolled down to the NAAFI when I spotted a familiar face. I walked over and just said 'Hello Sid', 'Blimey Binkie' he answered. Sid Harding was a mate of mine when I was with 3203 Servicing Commando. He told me how 3203 was involved with the North African landings 'Operation Torch' and later on with the invasion of Sicily and Italy. I had the distinct feeling he really didn't want to talk about it. He mentioned that 3203 only lost one chap out there. Apparently, 3203 was then disbanded and the personnel returned to England. I say apparently, because Sid was a bit vague and I didn't want to pursue the matter. I never saw Sid again after that evening.

Things were going pretty well as far as operations were concerned, but we did have one nasty shock, when Bill Waudby, one of the Wings most popular pilots was shot down over France. He was a huge man about six feet three inches tall with broad shoulders, a mop of unruly hair and an infectious grin. He was one of those chaps we thought would never be shot down, but there it was, but the good news was that he had baled out and as far as we know he landed safely, but more of that later.

It was now May 1944 and Win and I had wangled to get a short leave together. I said we, but I should have said she. I had written to her telling her of my leave. Now Win was at High Wycombe, Bomber Command Headquarters and was serving as a Batwoman to senior ranking officers. I don't know who, but she pulled a few strings about her boyfriend going on embarkation leave, and low and behold, she got her leave to coincide with mine.

The leave was wonderful, but Grays in Essex was like one huge military camp. Every sort of gun, lorry, and even tanks were secreted among the tree lined avenues, and as we walked around our streets and avenues it was more than obvious that the long awaiting invasion of Europe was imminent. As we walked homewards, I asked Win if we could get engaged before our leave was up. She was reluctant at first, saying something like 'shouldn't we wait a bit longer?' I pleaded with her, emphasising the fact that this was probably the last time we would see each other for a long time, because I knew that once I returned to camp, we would be preparing to embark for France. She thought for a while and then said, 'Yes, you are right'.

Then next day, we popped into Gurnett's the local jeweller for a ring, and to our amazement he said 'I'm afraid I can't offer you a selection, I only have one ring in the shop'. As luck would have it the ring fitted perfectly. It was a lovely ring of unusual design with a sapphire stone and after sixty years on Win's finger, it still looks great. Happily both sets of parents were delighted and said we had done the right thing.

Our leave over, we said a rather tearful farewell – not goodbye – and made our way back to our respective units. Back at Holmsley, there was so much speculation as to what was about to happen. There was more than the usual share of duff gen, although we were all ready to go, and the sooner the better for the uncertainty was making everyone edgy. Then one evening while we were in the NAAFI, the Tannoy blared out 'All 121 Wing personnel to report to their dispersals immediately'. We beetled off to our dispersals and found a large amount of paint tins and just as many brushes. We were then told to paint the wings and the tail unit of the aircraft with black and white stripes approximately 18-inches wide.

As we painted a procession of bombers started flying over, heading for the French coast. We knew then that 'it was on'. We were then told that the black and white stripes were for identification purposes for all allied aircraft taking part in the invasion and could be immediately identified by the stripes on the wings and tail units. All clever stuff, it was a bright idea but as luck would have it, Jerry never put in an appearance, or at least (as we were told later) only two Messerschmitt 109's bothered to do their best to spoil things.

All night long on the 5th June 1944, the continuous drone of aircraft engines rent the night sky. Sleep was out of the question, everyone on the ground said a silent prayer coupled with fervent wishes of good luck for those heroic lads in the bombers and gliders as they headed for the beaches of Normandy.

CHAPTER 7
Normandy Landings & operating from France

In the morning, we got the expected order, pack up ready to move. A short journey took us to Old Sarum, where we were paraded and told that we would be embarking within a day or so. Just to make sure all the drivers were instructed to make sure that their vehicles were in tip top condition. If anyone was unsure they would be issued with a new vehicle. Alan and I agreed that our Austin Power Tender was in fine fettle, so we never bothered. There must have been about a dozen or so drivers that thought they would take advantage of having new lorries. These drivers were all Bedford FWD Lorries and were nervous of the four wheel drive option. When the drivers returned with their new lorries we fell about laughing, for the new vehicles were the fearsome RAF Specials, a Thornicroft monstrosity designed for the RAF about 1926 and resembled the old General Buses that adorned the London streets in the 1910 to 1926 period.

One feature of the Special was its gearbox, it was said sarcastically, if you were going uphill and wanted to change down a gear, once in neutral, you could roll a fag while waiting for the revs to die down before you could engage the lower gear. Thank heaven I was never put in the position to find out.

Preparations were made for the impending embarkation and all the vehicles we had their engine and exhaust systems waterproofed. This entailed a flexible hose attached to the tail of the exhaust, which then went vertically up the back of the vehicle thus preventing water getting into the system, when disembarking from the landing ships onto the beach, assuming quite rightly that there would be four feet of water to negotiate, before hitting dry land. This waterproofing completed, we then drove to a marshalling area at Fareham, where we waited to embark.

The length of our wait was dependent on the Pioneer Corps and RAF Regiment preparing a makeshift airfield. This involved the laying of steel mesh wire on a suitable site. This we understood was to prevent aircraft sinking into the very soft sandy soil on Normandy.

The Pioneers and the RAF Engineers did a wonderful job in a very short space of time, as 121 Wing landed in Normandy on D Day Plus 6. Personally this was a very ignominious start, for as we drove down the ramp of the landing ship, we went straight into a shell hole. The landing ship had to reverse into the Channel again and make another attempt a few yards to one side. 'See the conqueror comes', went the old song. We had the worst possible start holding up the invasion, while we were towed out of the English Channel by a bulldozer. As it happens, no damage was done to our power tender, only our pride.

Once on dry land, we formed up in convoy and were escorted to our airstrip which was on the outskirts of a village named Camilly Sur Mur. If we expected a hero's welcome, we didn't get it. The few villagers we saw looked at us more as interlopers than liberators. The airstrip itself consisted of a couple of fields, one for the Station Headquarters, Field Kitchen, Sickbay etc.; and the main field was for dispersals and runway.

Our first order was to dig foxholes beside our tents close to the hedgerows. I should mention at this stage, that there was an incessant shelling by the Royal Navy on targets inland. This went on day and night for days on end.

Our aircraft arrived from England and after servicing and refuelling, we were told to use the camouflage netting and cover up the aircraft. We thought it was a barmy idea, as the grass was dry and discoloured like a newly mown cornfield, while the camouflage netting was dark green. We pointed out that the camouflaged aircraft stood out like a sore thumb, but orders were orders and had to be carried out. Our fears were confirmed when Jerry started to shell our airstrip. I can tell you that we were thankful that we had dug our foxholes. The shelling did no damage to speak of; just making holes all over the place, but it did make it very uncomfortable and limited our operations. It was then that we appreciated our skills in packing and moving on, for we were told just that. Pack ready to move which we did to another airfield at St. Croix. We had just got settled when Jerry let us know that he knew we were there, we were treated to another bout of shelling. Fortunately, there was no airfield at St. Croix, so no damage had been done. We then found out that our aircraft had flown back to bases in the U.K.

It was only a couple of days later that we returned to Camilly. Although the Germans had packed up shelling us, the Royal Navy was still pounding away at targets further inland. We grew accustomed to the guns firing and the shells whizzing overhead, then a very strange thing happened. One night, I would say sometime after midnight, the shelling stopped, just like that. You might think nothing wrong with that, but the sudden quiet woke everybody up. Bods were wandering about wondering what had happened, we could only assume that the army had embarked on some sort of advance. We never heard the naval guns again after that night.

Now that things had quietened down considerably, our aircraft returned to operate from Normandy again. Once we were operational again, it was like a taxi rank. The Army would get in touch by field telephone and inform us of a couple of Tiger Tanks or 88mm guns that they would like 'taken out'. Give us the position and our Typhoons would take off and duly oblige. It is rather remiss of me not to mention that before the invasion, our Typhoons were fitted with rockets and our pilots became so accurate with these weapons, that our army mates in the front line nicknamed them the 'Flying Winkle Pins'. Great credit however must go to the army and RAF personnel who worked together on the ground, pinpointing the targets with smoke bombs or star shells, showing our pilots exactly where their targets were.

It was during our stay at Camilly that I had the most terrifying experience of my life. The summer days were ideal for flying and we became used to seeing the large formations of American bombers going about their business. It got that we would hear aircraft engines, and we would look up and nonchantly say, 'oh, they are Boston's or Maryland's, but seldom did we see the 'big boys' like the Fortresses or Liberators, as they were employed in bashing enemy factories, oil installations and the like.

This particular day however, we looked up and saw a solitary Liberator limping towards home, the engines running rather erratic.

Suddenly, the crew started to bale-out, presumably they were in serious trouble and had decided to 'hit the silk' before they got over the Channel. We counted the chutes one by one and presumably the pilot before he too baled-out, had set 'George' to fly the plane; George being the nickname given to the automatic pilot. Whether or not 'George' didn't take kindly to being put in charge of a doomed aircraft, for after roughly two minutes the Liberator altered course.

Perhaps 'George' took a fancy to our airstrip or whether he thought it was party time and he would do his party piece, we didn't know, but he really put the fear of old nick into all of us on the ground. The aircraft was at about five thousand feet, when it suddenly put its nose down and came down in a vertical 'Stuka' like dive. Suddenly everyone started running for their lives, there was about 25-tons of aircraft coming straight down on us. Just as suddenly as it started to dive, 'George' pulled out of the dive; we didn't have to look, the sound of the engines told us that he was climbing again. The aircraft then stalled once more and once again he came diving straight at us. Bods began running everywhere. Talk about panic stations, no-one knew where they were running, they just ran and ran. At the last minute 'George' did his party piece again and started a spiral climb.

As we stood trying to get our breath back, 'George' levelled his kite again and coming round in a circular turn, he dived one more. This time, I promised to be a good boy, for surely it could not pull out of a dive for a third time?

If ever I experienced sheer terror, it was this. Running like the clappers, anywhere, but nowhere, just keep running. If you dared look up, he was coming straight for you. Again the painful snarl of the engines told us that he was climbing once more. A quick glance across the other side of the airstrip told us that the chaps over there were running too. This carried on for what seemed like an eternity, but in reality it was only a few minutes.

'George' decided he had had enough fun for one day, for the Liberator suddenly climbed and flew off in a southerly direction. Later that day, we were informed that the 'Yanks' sent a couple of their aircraft, P38 Lightnings after 'George', waited until he was over open pastures and shot it down.

Sixty years on and I can still relive the stark terror that I and all my mates experienced that day and say 'I thought the Yanks were on our side.' I didn't think much of them on that day.

At last things started to go right for the invading forces, both the British and Americans were gaining ground. Then one evening, the Tannoys blared out, 'all squadrons released.' This was most unusual, for we were at 'readiness' every night until dusk, when we had to' cover up' for the night. This particular evening however the Tannoys blared out again. 'If you look to the north-east you will see something of interest.' He wasn't kidding, for suddenly we saw them, hundreds and hundreds of Lancasters, Halifaxes and Wimpey's, Bostons, you name them and they were there.

We were about to witness the 1,000 bomber raid on Caen and we had ringside seats.

The sky was literally black with aircraft, but the frightening thing about it was the co-ordinating of so many aircraft appearing at the same time. We stood, excited, amazed, but at the same time thinking 'God help those poor sods who would be underneath that lot.' We watched until the last plane had turned for home. We had witnessed the raid and we had only seen one Lancaster shot down. Wonderful!

Relations with the army were never better than they were now, and someone had the bright idea of inviting the lads coming back from the front line for a rest. The army boys were thrilled to see the 'Flying Winkle Pins' and inevitably they would ask 'can we sit in the cockpit? I had to laugh when one squaddie made the request and asked a rigger for a particular aircraft, who said 'sure you can, but take them bleeding great boots off first, I don't want you scratching it.'

I explained to another squaddie that no offence was meant, but if he looked around he would see that the majority of 'erks' were wearing Gum boots for the sole reason of not scratching the aircraft. He muttered something like 'and we thought our sergeant major was fussy.' All in all, the army lads were full of praise for the work our 'Tiffies' were doing, adding 'thank God they are on our side.'

Off to War! Pictured soon after completing my training, back in Grays with some of the local lads: Left to right Henry & Les Vidler, Myself, seated John Brinkley & his nephew.

Hawkinge 1941: left to right 'Tiny', 'Taffy' Evans & 'Wacker' Kirk with
myself in cockpit. R. Bayford Collection

One of my pencil drawings of 91ˋ Squadron's Spit's done at Hawkinge.
Ron Bayford Collection

Squadron Leader Ray Harries who commanded No. 91 Squadron, he become one of the outstanding fighter pilots and Wing leaders during WW2.
Copyright IWM CH 13599

Flight Lieutenant J.J. Le Roux pictured in the cockpit of his Spitfire. He was another excellent and formidable fighter pilot who flew with 91 Squadron. Unfortunately, like so many others, he did not survive the war.
Copyright IWM CL 784

The French pilot Jean Demozay, known as 'Moses' to us at Hawkinge.
He became an ace with the squadron and eventually notched up 21
victories by wars end.

Johnny Heap poses by his Spitfire. Johnny was tragically killed in 1944, when his damaged aircraft crashed on return from operations.
Richard C. Smith Collection

Pilots of 'A' Flight 91 Squadron pictured at Lympne: L/R 'Scotty' Downer, Jules De Molene, Ron Ingram, Johnny Heap, Bill Orr, Bobby Oxspring, Frank Silk, Bob Spurdle, the Adj, Johnny Edwards, Sammy Hall & John Lambert. Richard C. Smith Collection

A Lysander MkIII A, belonging to No. 277 Air Sea Rescue Squadron RAF, preparing for a practice sortie from Hawkinge in Kent. Seen here with an M-Type dinghy containers fitted on the undercarriage stub wings and smoke floats on the rear bomb-racks. Copyright IWM CH 7571

Another of my doddles, showing the 91 Squadron 'Jim Crow' cartoon of which we were very proud.   Ron Bayford Collection

Ground crew of 'A' Flight prepare their 91 Squadron Spitfires for another sortie from Hawkinge.   Richard C. Smith Collection

American built Alligator amphibious transporters hit the beach during Commando Servicing Unit exercises at Inverary in Scotland 1942. Copyright IWM H 25486

Pilots of No. 245 Squadron walk past their Hawker Typhoon Mk1Bs to their dispersal hut at Westhampnett. Three of the Typhoons wear cowling covers with 'chimneys' for the insertion of a heater, in order to aid the engine start. Copyright IWM CH 12255

Some of the ground crew enjoying a game of cricket as other service a Hawker Typhoon of 174 Squadron outside a canvas hangar at B5, Camilly, Normandy, 7th July 1944.   Copyright IWM CL 407

A section of Hawker Typhoons of 175 Squadron take off from airfield B5 at Camilly, watched by armourers at work on another Typhoon of No. 245 Squadron, July 1944.   Copyright IWM CL 449

Prime Minister Winston Churchill secretly arrives at our airfield at Camilly, flown in by a captured Fiesler Storch aircraft flown by Harry 'Broady' Broadhurst of 2nd T.A.F.
Richard C. Smith Collection

Ground crew loading 3-inch Rocket projectiles, onto a Hawker Typhoon Mk1B at airfield B2 Bazenville in Normandy.
Copyright IWM CL 157

Camilly Sur Mur, Normandy, France
1944: Myself, Bill Waudby and 'Taffy'
Evans.   R. Bayford Collection

Playing my beloved Gibson guitar,
Douvai, France 1944.
R. Bayford Collection

Douvai, France 1944: L/R Fred Soden
with dog, Jimmy Walker & Bill Sale.
R. Bayford Collection

Ground crew servicing and refuelling a Hawker Tempest in flooded
conditions, after heavy rain at Volkel, Holland on 29th November 1944.
Copyright IWM CLC 1676

Dutch workmen repair a dispersal area at the airfield at Volkel in Holland.
In the background ground crew service a Hawker Tempest.
Copyright IWM CL 1415

'Yours truly' at Volkel, winter 1944. 'Too bloody cold for my liking.'
Ron Bayford Collection

Spring 1945: Back Row: Stan King, Jimmy Walker, Bill Moseley, Myself, Front Row: Alan Hemmings, 'Taffy' Evans & Fred Soden.   Ron Bayford Collection

Volkel, Holland, spring 1945: Back Row: Brin Jones, myself, unknown. Front Row: Jimmy Walker, Fred Soden, unknown.
Ron Bayford Collection

Volkel 1945: Pictured in front of one of our 245 Squadron Typhoon aircraft. L/R Bill Moseley, Stan King & 'Taffy' Evans.   Ron Bayford Collection

A Hawker Tempest Mk V, of No. 274 Squadron, begins its take-off run at B80 aerodrome at Volkel, Holland.

Copyright IWM FLM 1464

Four members of the famous RAF 'Squadronaires' band playing during a broadcast from the BBC studios in the Paris Cinema, London on 16th April 1945. The pianist Ronny Aldrich is in the foreground; the other musicians are Sid Colin on guitar, Jock Cummings on drums and Arthur Madden on double bass.

Copyright IWM CH 15079

'Taffy' Evans with Squadron Leader Schweiberg seated in cockpit, and unknown groundcrewman, Volkel 1945. Ron Bayford Collection

Win in her WAAF uniform whilst serving at Bomber Command Headquarters, High Wycombe, Buckinghamshire.
Ron Bayford Collection

Win and myself on our Wedding Day at the Aveley Chapel, 7th April 1945.
R. Bayford Collection

My last view of the war as our
ship departs from Ostend,
Belgium, August 1945.
R. Bayford Collection

We had the chance to forget the war for a few hours, when we were told that a Liberty Wagon was going into Bayeux. This was a welcome break and naturally we made our way to the Cathedral to see the tapestry. The visit was spoilt for me when, although minding my own business, a Nun came over and gave me a lot of verbal. I don't know what for and I thought of saying 'and up yours too! But I thought better of it, gave a mock bow and murmured 'Pardon Madam' (I didn't know the French for Nun or Sister) so she had to make do.

Once outside the Cathedral, I was shocked to see how many WAAFs and WRACs there were already in Normandy. Seeing the girls in uniform and the civilians all walking about in the sunshine, made it very hard to believe there was a war going on just up the road.

When I got back to the airstrip, there was a great deal of excitement and I asked what it was all about. The answer was 'Look whose is over there.' It was Bill Waudby, the pilot who was shot down a few weeks previously. He was surrounded by pilots and erks, all wanting to know how he had found his way back to us.

His story was simple enough, but it was more like something out of a Biggles yarn. He baled-out successfully and when he landed, he hid in the woods nearby and buried his parachute. He eventually found some friendly villagers who spirited him away to the local resistance, the Maquis. He insisted on joining them and apparently enjoyed himself blowing up trains, German staff cars and the like. When he learned of the invasion, he found out through the grapevine that there was an airstrip at Camilly, with Typhoons operating from there. With the help of his French friends, he found his way back to us.

Now he was back, all he wanted was to get back into action. This was not to be however, for Intelligence had found out that the Germans had put a price on his head, and although he was still in the RAF and still able to fly, he was forbidden to fly on the continent in case he was shot down again and captured, in which case Bill would face the firing squad.

A few days later we again had an early release and all the squadrons stood down. Again the Tannoy advised us to look out for something interesting and sure enough, we saw another air armada approaching, hundreds and hundreds of them, the same mix of Lancasters, Halifaxes etc, all homing in on one target. The ground shook with thousands upon thousands of explosions as the bombs rained down. They were much closer to us than the previous raid on Caen. We learnt afterwards that it was Villers Bocage, a tiny village that Jerry had turned into a fortress. I couldn't help thinking to myself, 'I bet the bomber boys thought that was a bit of a doddle, having a soft target for a change, instead of the horrendous jobs they usually got, flying hundreds of miles through constant barrages of flak and attacks by night-fighters.

Then came the day when we on 245 Squadron were shaken rigid. Our commanding officer, Squadron Leader Jack Collins had been hit when making an attack on an enemy position, he baled-out, but it went horribly wrong, for his parachute got caught on his tailplane and he went down with his stricken aircraft. We were all devastated by his death and the manner in which he died. It hit me hard for an incident had taken place a few days earlier. It was at a time when the Luftwaffe had an ace called Mantoni. This pilot had been shot down on the same day that Jack Collins had bagged a Jerry. We were congratulating Jack Collins on his 'kill' and one of the erks happened to ask him 'Do you think that it was Mantoni Sir? Jack answered 'I don't know anything about Mantoni, I know more about Mantovani and he hasn't got anything on Binkie here.' That was his reference to my guitar playing. I was full of pride at that reference, but the more so, was that he knew me, even my nickname. I have treasured that all my life.

Our new commanding officer arrived, Squadron Leader Schweiberg, an English/Swiss national, whom we found out that in civilian life had been a pilot for Swiss Air. We took to him straight away and one of the first things he wanted was someone to paint Sharks teeth on the front of his aircraft. I think it was a chap named Cakebread who did the job for him. I must say it was a fearsome looking monster, when the painting had been completed. As it turned out our own 'Flying Tiger' stayed like that until the end of the war.

There was one particular incident at Camilly that I will always cherish. The entire Wing was paraded in an annexe field with trees on three sides. We all wondered what it was all about, our pilots didn't know, the NCOs didn't, but we had to remain in ranks and wait. We did exactly that and then heard an aircraft approaching. Looking up we saw a Feisler Storch, a German spotter plane. Then the order went up 'Parade Attention.' The Storch glided down and as the cockpit was of the greenhouse type, we could see who was in it. Everyone recognised the hunched figure dressed in black with a familiar Bowler hat. The shout went up 'Its Winnie.' We forgot we were at attention, the cheers went up and our FS caps were waved. It was our boss Winston Churchill. As the Storch turned into our parade and came to a halt, the door opened and 'Winnie' alighted, all smiles, Cigar in place and waving his famous Bowler hat.

He signalled us to be quiet and made a brief speech. He told us how pleased he was to be in Normandy and said he was delighted with the way things were going. He praised the work our 'Tiffies' were doing and told us he was never more sure that victory would be ours. As he prepared to leave, he turned briefly to shake hands with our commanding officer Tim Morice. The lads cheered at this gesture, and I don't know who could have been more proud, Tim Morice, or me, who had the privilege of seeing our 'guv' Winston Churchill.

After the plane had taken off, a thought struck me, had Tim Morice and Winston met before? After all, Tim was a First World War hero with many decorations. Could it be that Tim had been decorated at an investiture when Winston was there? How proud he must have been to meet both his Majesty the King and Winston Churchill. I know that the erks were very proud of our CO, I would go as far as to say they idolised him.

By now, things were going extremely well for the Allies. The Americans had captured Boulogne and Caen had eventually fallen. An entire German army was now squeezed into a small pocket, with just a small gap for some of them to escape. The now famous Falaise gap closed shut. Although Adolf Hitler ordered his generals to fight to the last man, the generals refused and subsequently surrendered. I shall never forget the sight of thousands of German prisoners of war, shuffling slowly past our airstrip on their way to the beaches for transportation to England for internment.

With the Germans now in full flight, our squadrons were ordered to attack anything that moved heading towards Germany. Tanks, lorries, horse and carts all fell victim to our Typhoons. One pilot in particular, Pilot Officer 'Spike' Hughes was a Lay Preacher in civilian life, a quiet inoffensive man, but his fellow pilots called him a callous killer when he was in the cockpit. One pilot told us that Spike had attacked a single German on a bicycle; such was his intense hatred of the Nazis.

It was now time for us to do what we were trained to do. Pack up and move. In the shortest possible time we were on the move to St. Andre. This was probably the shortest stay we had at any time and no sooner had we arrived, than we were told to make for Beauvais. This name brought back memories to me, for I remembered the disastrous flight of the Airship R101. This was the airship which had taken off against the advice from experts, who claimed the ship was not ready to fly. At least that was what we were told. However, the airship took off, crossed the English Channel and slowly lost height until she crashed into a hill at Beauvais.

We now assumed that we were out of Normandy, for the locals made us really welcome. We were invited into people's homes and this was rather funny; wherever we were invited we were always confronted by a huge Custard pie. Honestly, I have never had so many Custard pies in all my life.

The other main difference from Normandy was the whole layout of the countryside. Whereas Normandy was mainly 'Bocage' country, this being made up of small fields surrounded by hedgerows, we now saw rolling fields more like the English South Downs.

At this stage of the invasion, the 2nd Tactical Air Force began to exercise its strategy. In our own particular case, 121 Wing and our sister 124 Wing, began our leapfrog operations. We would be at X airfield, and as the army advanced, 124 would leap frog over us to keep up with the army (as I already explained, we were mainly army support Wings), then as the army advanced further, we in turn would leapfrog over 124 Wing. In this manner, both Wings would have breathing space between moves. The army was now advancing so fast that we were being 'pushed' keeping up with them.

The advance rate was now so great, that problems began to mount up with supplies not keeping up, so now 121 Wing embarked on a new, but temporary role. We had moved to an airfield at Douai, which was near Lille. After having unloaded and erected everything that had to be erected, we were called together by Wing Commander Tim Morice, who informed us that we were temporarily non-operational. He then told us that because of the supplies problem, starting tomorrow, supplies would be flown in from England by Dakota aircraft of both the RAF and USAAF and we would have the task of unloading them. How jolly!

We were woken by Tannoy at dawn and formed into sections. An army NCO was allocated and a senior NCO (probably a Sergeant Major) supervised the whole operation. If you had been told how much a Dakota can carry, I would never have believed them. Once the aircraft had taxied to its directed dispersal, the door would open and we formed a chain gang passing ammunition, petrol, oil, guns, you name it, we shifted it. Waiting lorries were in turn loaded and then off they would jolly well go. Streuth! I never knew so many Dakotas existed. The taxi rank was endless. They would land, unload, taxi around the perimeter track and take off home for some more goodies. Did I say goodies? Well, in some cases we did get some. The USAAF crews were very good to us, sometimes they would give us some cigarettes, chocolates, tins of fruit etc., 'Don't worry buddy, there are stacks of these at our PX.' This was their equivalent to our NAAFI, but it was more plentiful and more superior. (Who on earth ever got a tin of pineapple from the NAAFI?)

After a few days of this we were really 'cream crackered' and we were glad when there was a slight lull in the proceedings. Our tent was pitched just inside the barbed wire which was just inside the airfield which separated the airfield from the road and one evening at dusk, approaching our tent I saw a young lady standing in the road. She called out 'Good evening' and I answered 'Good evening Madam' and she asked if I was English. I said that I was and complimented her on how well she spoke English. She laughed and said something like, 'It's because I am an English woman and come from Brighton'. She told me she had married a Frenchman before the war and came with him to live at a place named Douai. He was called up for the French Army and was a prisoner of war. She went on to say how badly they had fared under the German occupation troops and how they either stole all the food, or made sure that they were first to get whatever was going. Brute force was the order of the day, punishment was made at the least excuse, emphasising that disobedience was punishable by death. She also said that she lived in fear, in case the Germans discovered that she was English.

By this time, 'Rog Rogers' and Bill Sale had joined us and they listened with me as she told us about life under German rule and thanked us for liberating them. We asked her if food supplies had reached Douai and she shook her head. We then asked her if she could come back the following evening, so that we could talk some more. She said that she could, and would be pleased to talk to her own countrymen.

When she had gone, Rog, Bill and I put our heads together and had a whip around among the erks who had learned of our lady's plight. The lads had contributed tins of Corned Beef, tinned Vegetables, Chocolate, tinned fruit and other goodies we had acquired from our Yankee friends who flew the Dakotas. We near enough filled a kit bag with these gifts, and when our lady came that evening, we had to ask her if she lived very far away from the airfield. When she indicated that she only lived about half a mile down the road, we then asked her if she had a perambulator. She was a bit taken aback when we asked her if she could go back and get it. This she did and looking slightly embarrassed asked us why we wanted it. When she saw the bag of food she broke down and cried. When she recovered, she could not believe what we had given her. They had not seen Corned Beef or anything else for years, and said she would share the food with her friends. She went away thanking God, the English, the RAF and Winston Churchill.

We saw her again a couple of evenings later, she called out from the roadway and after we had exchanged a few pleasantries, she held out a small bag saying 'This is from our friends, it isn't much, but it is all we can give you.' We accepted the bag under protest and in it perhaps were a dozen eggs and some tomatoes. We were a bit choked to think they had been so generous when they had so little to give. Needless to say we gave her a few more goodies in exchange.

After she had gone, I reflected on how different these people were from those in Normandy. There, the farmers refused to sell us a few new potatoes which were growing abundantly in the surrounding fields. At the same time they encouraged their children to accost us for 'Cigarette for Papa' or 'Chocolate for my Sister.' Other than that, they seemed to resent our presence, almost to being belligerent. They didn't treat us as liberators, but more as interlopers. That was the opinion we formed anyway.

Although we were still engaged in our task of unloading our supplies from the never ending stream of Dakotas, we were now able to go into Douai after we had been released. We were instructed never to go alone, so Rog, Jimmy, Bill and I decided we would go into town together.

We went into Douai complete with Rifle, Gas Mask and Steel Helmet just in case. We were surprised to see how many French Maquis there were on the streets, all armed. We conversed to them the best way we could, but we never ever asked them where they got their arms from. One chap however, warned us that if we were returning to camp after dark, should we be challenged, we were to stop at once and answer something like 'Anglais, RAF, Mon Ami'.

The second time in Douai, we were approached by a young French girl who in broken English asked if we would like to come to her house to meet Mamma and Papa to have a cup of coffee. This we accepted and we duly met her parents. Her father had fought against the Germans during the Great War and really hated them. Marguerite, as we now knew her, acted as interpreter, so we got on rather well. Through Marguerite her mother asked me if I were a pilot, I told her I was a Penguin. When Marguerite gave her my answer, all the family looked baffled and puzzled and asked what I meant. I simply said, 'I didn't fly.' Marguerite giggled and translated my answer and the family roared with laughter. I didn't think it was particularly funny, but they thought it was hilarious and kept calling me 'Penguin'. When they found out that I played the piano and guitar, they went into fits of laughter saying 'le musicale Penguin!'

Marguerite played the piano a bit and her father asked her to sing. I wish he hadn't because it was horrible. She had this peculiar thin, tinny wavering voice which seemed to be the norm in French females and when she started to sing, I could see Jimmy, Bill and Rog sitting there squirming with embarrassment, doing their best not to laugh. When she had finished her torturous concert, we courteously clapped, but curiously not one of us asked for an encore. Then she asked me to play something jolly, so I played and my own male voice choir gave our rendition of 'Pistol Packing Mama'.

The family thought it was great and I had to keep on playing it until they could join in, 'Lay that pistol down babe, lay that pistol down'. I then played a couple of French love songs that I knew and again they sang with great gusto.

After two or three evenings at Marguerite's house, Bill became rather attached to one of Marguerite's friends, and we could see that she felt the same way about him. She was different from Marguerite, as she was very dark complexion with Black hair and Brown eyes, whereas Marguerite was fair haired with Blue yes, but not as pretty as her friend. However, she (I can't recall her name) would sit and gaze at Bill, all gooey eyed, and it came as no surprise when Bill asked her, (through Marguerite) if he could take her out, to which she readily agreed. I might be a bit thick, but for the life of me I couldn't see how they could converse, as Bill couldn't speak French, and she couldn't speak English.

I got on quite well with Marguerite until Papa asked me (again through Marguerite) if I was married. I then became a bit uneasy for when I said that I was single, she asked me if I 'ad Fiancée?' I told her that I did have a fiancée; I could tell that both she and 'papa' were disappointed. I felt a bit rotten about it, but I had to tell the truth – I just couldn't 'string her along'.

Our friendship with the French family came to an end, when out of the blue, came the all too familiar order 'pack up, ready to move'. We left Douai with some regrets, but the war was still going on, and we did have the satisfaction of knowing that our stint of unloading supplies from the Dakotas went a long way to keep our troops supplied with their needs.

We passed into Belgium, and it was very gratifying to see the happiness and joy the Belgian people showed as we passed through the towns and villages. We eventually arrived at our new 'home' in Antwerp. We were not too happy to learn that the Germans still occupied part of Antwerp, but we had to put up with it. There were dense woods or forest a couple of miles away from our airfield, and Jerry still occupied part of them – as we soon found out.

CHAPTER 8
Belgium, Holland & the Ardennes

We all knew how vital Antwerp was to both us and also to the Germans. If we could capture the Port itself, then the problem of supplies would ease considerably. Whilst the Americans enjoyed the luxury of having the Port of Cherbourg to use, the British were still relying on supplies being unloaded at the Mulberry Harbour and then ferried by road to the front line, so it would be a massive prize to capture Antwerp Port and the approaches, so that we could get our supplies direct.

We (121 Wing) started operations straight away giving our forward troops the air support they needed, and things began to look rosy, but then the Germans retaliated by attacking our airfield with 88mm guns concealed in the overlooking woods. They would fire perhaps a dozen rounds – just enough to disrupt us, then move away to another part of the woods to fire another few rounds. Although we employed 'spotter' planes to cover the woods, they never seemed to find the enemy guns. This went on for a few days (and nights) as he would wait until the early hours and let loose a few rounds, so our night's sleep was disturbed, and leaving us edgy and nervous, for a canvas tent was not much shelter from an 88mm shell! As it happened I cannot recall anyone being hit by these shells, but all the same we had the '88 twitch'.

It was at this time, that I almost 'had my chips' for I was just leaving the field kitchen area, when Jerry opened up and let loose the usual few rounds, and I threw myself into a small divot in the field. It was then that a shell burst close by, and the blast whipped my steel helmet off. Luckily I had the helmet strap at the back of my head – if I had the strap under my chin I would probably have been decapitated. After the shelling I never, ever saw my helmet again. Although I was issued with a new one, it was not the same. I was proud of my old helmet with old 'Jim Crow' painted on the front. To me, it was unique for none of my pals at 91 Squadron had bothered to paint Jim Crow on their helmets. Whoever found my helmet would never know the significance of the painting of a Crow in a top hat with a bow tie, waistcoat and an umbrella under his wing.

We had been operating from Antwerp for some time, when another unforgettable thing happened. We were all going about our tasks when we heard the sound of aircraft. We knew at once by the sound it was a large formation, and as it came into view we saw hundreds of aircraft, each one towing a Glider. 'Crikey!' We thought something big is happening here. We didn't know it at the time, but we were witnessing the air armada going to the now famous air invasion at Arnhem. To a man we stood and waved and cheered as these brave Paratroopers headed to Arnhem, but as we cheered, we had no idea of the disaster that awaited them. For as long as I live, I will never forget the sight of that air armada.

It was at Antwerp that something else happened, that I will never forget. One day we heard a strange sort of aero engine, and when we looked up someone shouted 'It's on fire', sure enough, flames were coming from its rear, then suddenly the engine cut, and we watched it dive, or rather fluttered down out of sight. A loud explosion followed, and we assumed that this strange looking aircraft had been carrying a bomb, but then we reasoned it was too small to carry a bomb, for it looked like a very small fighter, or pursuit plane.

Shortly afterwards we heard another of these strange machines, and again flames were coming from its rear. This time however, it did not crash, but just kept on flying until it was out of sight. We were more than concerned when yet another of these weird machines came into sight, with 'its arse on fire'. They came over in spasms, and we began to ask questions like, 'Why do they come over singly, and not in squadrons' and 'How or why do some of them crash and others go straight on' or 'Are they some sort of Kamikaze jobs like the Japs have been using?' Then one of them had barely cleared our airfield when the engine cut, and again it fluttered down to earth. We saw quite clearly that it wasn't carrying a bomb, but then there was this deafening explosion. 'What the bloody hell was that, then if it wasn't a bomb' someone shouted. By now, we weren't concerned; we were frightened, because we didn't know what it was coming at us. They tailed off towards the evening, and eventually stopped – or rather we thought they had, for they started coming over again the next day. Then we were officially notified that the mysterious 'things' were one of Hitler's secret 'victory weapons' and were referred to as V1's. I can assure you, that was not what we called them. We were then told that these weapons were primarily being used against Antwerp (which we already knew) and Brussels, but some of them were being directed against Southern England and London. These 'Doodle-bugs' as they were now known were difficult to shoot down because of their speed, but the fighter pilots in England had hit on the idea of getting above them when they spotted them and dived attaining enough speed to catch them and firing at them, while some of the pilots preferred to catch them and tip them over with their wings.

It was not a happy period in my life in the RAF, what with being shelled by the German 88s and being under threat from the Doodle Bugs, whilst servicing our aircraft. However, that was our job and we had to do it however nerve racking it was. We thought of our own pilots who were being shot up by Ack-Ack guns and risking being attacked by Me109s every time they went up. We realised that we had it cushy compared to them.

As late Autumn set in, we were given the order to get ready to pack up and move, and to be honest we were somewhat relieved to be moving away from Antwerp; that was until we were told that we would have to run the gauntlet up the corridor, a section of Belgium where our troops had driven a wedge in the German defences and were now racing to capture the coast line where the Doodle Bugs were being launched. This meant our convoy route was directed straight through the German lines and could be subjected to enemy fire from both sides of the road.

Bloody charming we thought, especially we were told that the convoy trucks would be well spaced out and when we reached a certain 'check point' the military police would then tell us to put our 'toe down' and go full pelt up the corridor, under no circumstances would we stop, except if we were hit by a shell fire. I remember saying to myself' put your foot down and go like the clappers,' in my

Power Tender, which being mounted on top of an ambulance chassis, would sway like 'Kelly's Cottage' when it reached 28 mph on a straight, properly surfaced road. What on earth would the old girl do if I drove like the clappers on a pock marked dirt road? To be honest, I didn't even try to go faster than the old girl was used to. Even then the howls and shouts coming from the back of the vehicle were bad enough and more than once I thought the old girl was going to tip over. As it happened, Jerry was very kind to us, and only fired the odd round or two during our mad dash.

When we eventually came to the end of the corridor, we found ourselves in Holland, and to our surprise we had to keep going. When we passed Eindhoven, we thought 'Crickey' at this rate we shall soon be in Berlin. At long last we found ourselves at a simply vast airfield named Volkel. It was the biggest airfield I have ever been on (I was never in Bomber Command where the airfields stretched for miles). We settled down and some of our 'bods' were lucky enough to be accommodated in some sort of Nissen hut, whilst the rest of us had to kip down in our tents.

It was soon back to business with our squadrons giving our forward troops the air cover they needed, taking out guns and tanks that were making a nuisance of themselves. Winter set in early at Volkel and some snow did its best to hinder operations. As it happened, someone had the foresight to amass a stockpile of shovels and stiff brooms, so we aided the civilian workers who were employed by us, managed to keep our main runway reasonably clear. At this point I must mention as an added incentive, the civilian workers were allowed to join us at the Field Kitchen during mealtimes.

It shook us something rotten when they joined us with just one tin plate or tin, whereas we had two mess tins. I could not believe it when a chap in front of me held out his plate for the inevitable 'Machonicies and potatoes' and then indicated to the cook to put his rice on the same plate. As he sat down, I was amazed to see him stir his rice and his main meal and woof it down with great gusto. Now and again he would stop to say 'Goot' and then finish his demolition job on his dinner. It soon dawned on us that the Dutch people had been virtually starved.

Wonders will never cease, or at least that is what we have always been led to believe, but one day at Volkel, Sergeant Bob Davis approached me and asked 'How long have you been an AC1?' I scratched my head and thought for a while and said something like 'I don't really know it has been so long, I have forgotten.' Bob went on to say that SHQ had received instructions that the appropriate personnel could be tested for upgrading. They had some posh word for it, but the meaning was the same.

I can remember saying to Bob that it would be a waste of time, for if I was upgraded to LAC, I knew from the past, that I would have to answer questions on bombsights and other instruments that you would find on Bomber aircraft. I emphasised to him that I hadn't even seen a bombsight or a gyroscopic compass since I had left training school in 1941, nearly four years ago, so I've got no chance of passing. 'Look Binkie' he said ' I have known you for two years, ever since I came to 121 Wing and I know and everyone else knows that you know your job inside out and I can remember when you once had to look after the whole squadron single handed, so I know you deserve your props.' 'Thanks Sarge' I can remember saying, 'but that won't carry much weight with the bod who gives me the test.' He replied 'Oh yes it will because Pilot Officer Pearson in charge of Electrical and Instruments has detailed me to give you the test, because he doesn't know anything about instruments.'

He gave me a few routine questions and said 'Right I am recommending you for the rank of Leading Aircraftsman, OK?

It was a lovely feeling sewing my props on my tunic, but what Bob had not told me was he had been promoted to flight sergeant and that Bill Leach, Alan Hemmings, Eddie Grant and 'Ham' Hammond had all been promoted from corporal to sergeant. No wonder Bob Davis was so easy about me getting my 'props.' Sometime later I reflected on what he had said about me and I wondered whether it was a bit of old flannel or was he genuine? I like to think it was the latter, because Bob was a good type.

We got on well with the locals, and I can remember one chap when I asked him 'What is that building over there? He replied that it was a Monastery and added with a grin, that the other building nearby was a Nunnery. He added that 'They think we don't know, but there is a connecting tunnel between the two buildings.' He grinned and nodded his head as if to say 'and you know what for – don't you.' Here endeth the first lesson. By now you must have guessed that English was the second language spoken by Dutch people.

One day the word went around. 'Heard the latest gen? Jerry has cut us off and they are talking about evacuating us by Dakota, while our pilots fly our kites back to a base in Belgium.' No one seemed to know if this was true, the NCO had heard nothing; the officers were tight lipped. All we did know was that Hertogenbosch, a town just a few miles down the road, had been retaken by the Germans, so we reasoned that it could be true about being airlifted out. Happily it never materialised, so it was business as usual.

December arrived and with came the bad weather. It was bitterly cold, with plenty of cold wet snow. We worked hard keeping our runway cleared and as it happened, it was a Godsend that we did, for we heard on the Forces Network Radio, that the Germans had broken through the Ardennes and that the Yanks were in full retreat.

This was the sort of news we could have done without, for we knew that the USAAF were grounded because of the snow and fog. This meant that the American troops had no air cover whatsoever and we didn't have the means to stop the Tiger tanks and 88s. We also knew that if the Americans lost Bastogne, the Germans would have a clear run straight through to Antwerp. We would have been right 'up the Swanee' in other words; the British would have been completely cut off.

General Eisenhower acted swiftly and put General Montgomery in complete command of the English and American troops in that sector. This had an immediate effect on us, for we the 2nd TAF were to give the Americans the air cover they so desperately needed, whilst their own aircraft were out of action due to weather conditions. To be honest, I don't know how it affected other units, but we worked nonstop right through the period running up to Christmas, through Christmas Eve, Christmas and Boxing Day. All squadrons 174,175, 184 and 245, were continually airborne, attacking targets that the Americans wanted 'taking out' and invariably our 'Flying Winklepins' obliged.

History tells the rest, Bastogne was held, the fog suddenly lifted, reinforcements arrived for the Americans and suddenly the spectre of a disastrous defeat was gone. The tables were turned and the Germans were back where they started.

While we were congratulating ourselves over the failure of 'Jerry's last throw, he then did his best to commit suicide. On New Year's Eve, the Luftwaffe decided to come out to play and threw everything he had at the 2nd Tactical Air Force. The Germans attacked airfields in Holland, Belgium and France, in another attempt to kill off our air forces. Although, he had a measure of success in destroying hundreds of our aircraft on the ground, he suffered enormous losses himself, aircraft he could never replace; whilst our own squadrons were back to full strength in a matter of days.

One incident occurred at Volkel during this 'last' fling of the Luftwaffe, was when we were being strafed by three Messerschmitt 109s, just as a flight of Hawker Tempests were returning to base. From our 'foxholes' we could see the Tempests approaching, undercarts down, flaps down ready to land. Suddenly the flaps and undercarriages went back up, as the Messerschmitts turned for another strike; the Tempests opened up and shot down all the 109s. They were now three heaps of burning rubbish, cluttering the place up. It was fantastic how quickly the Tempest pilots had reacted and shot the 109s down, all in a matter of seconds.

As the day drew to a close and things began to get back to normal, we heard that our sister Wing, No124 had been clobbered at Eindhoven and had suffered quite a few casualties. This was confirmed a couple of days later, when our adjutant told us how many of the erks had been killed. I was deeply shocked when I learnt that my old mate 'Blondie' Beckett was among those lost. My mind went back to the first days at Wrexham, when George Stubbs and I were joined in our tent by the two 'townies' 'Smokey' Box and 'Blondie' Becket. We four stuck together for some time, until 'Smokey' was transferred owing to his age and 'Blondie' was posted to 124 Wing.

Things quietened down after Jerry's disastrous attempt to destroy the Allied Air Forces and we were delighted when some of our pilots, four I believe, were awarded the American Silver Star for their part in the Battle of the Bulge. We were also told that several 'erks' were mentioned in despatches, by ballot, or so we were told, but somehow no one seemed to know who these chaps were, not even by my mate George Edwards who worked in the Orderly Room.

In retrospect, it seemed rather strange that in spite of these gongs being awarded. No mention was ever made of the Typhoons contributions in destroying the bulk of the enemy armour, whilst the American Air Force was unable to get off the ground.

I have read umpteen books, watched documentaries and official films, but nowhere has the Typhoon been mentioned; if it has it must have been very much glossed over, but the fact is we were there assisting the Americans. Perhaps it was because the Americans were too embarrassed to admit that we did what they couldn't.

Back to our troubles at Volkel, for now owing to the flat nature of Holland's terrain, the snow as it began to melt flooded our 'Foxholes' on the dispersals and became full of water; so they were absolutely useless should the German's attempt to have another go at strafing.

As far as personnel were concerned, we had two new chaps on 245, Freddie Soden and Corporal Moseley. We were amazed when Freddie made himself known, for he produced a pet Rabbit from under his battledress tunic and simply said 'this is Slash, he goes everywhere with me.' How on earth he managed to smuggle 'Slash' out of the UK and all the way to Holland, goodness knows. It was so funny, but as soon as 'Slash' was introduced to 'Tiffie' our pet cat, they became inseparable.

Bill Moseley on the other hand was a loner; he would never speak unless someone spoke to him first. He was best described as someone put it, as bit of a funny bugger.

We eventually found out that in Civvy Street Bill was a Lay Preacher. He didn't smoke, drink anything other than tea or water, never swore and never mentioned girls or women. He never divulged whether he was married. Freddie said sarcastically 'I bet he didn't even have a Mother, he's that sort of bloke.' Poor Bill, he was not exactly a barrel of laughs. As much as he was an outsider, no one ever took the mickey out of him. When he said Grace at meal times, or when he said his prayers at night, everyone kept quiet. It was the way he chose to lead his life and it was none of our business.

He only upset us once and that was when the Germans let loose their Me262 Jet propelled aircraft on us. At first we hadn't a clue about them, for one day just as the 'take cover' sirens were going, there was a few small explosions followed by a 'whooshing' sound in the sky. We looked up and saw nothing. Then we were told that Jerry had these Jet propelled kites that could fly faster than the speed of sound. This explained why they had dropped their bombs and were away before we actually heard them. To add to this, our intelligence people told us that they had dropped Anti-Personnel bombs, which exploded about fifty feet in the air, throwing shrapnel downwards instead of sideways. This meant diving down a foxhole would be absolutely useless. All we could hope to do now, was to wear our 'Battle Bowlers' all the time and hope for the best.

Despite all of this, our aircraft had to be serviced and so we went about our tasks the best we could. Some of us scrounged an odd piece of corrugated tin sheeting that could give us some sort of cover to our foxholes. Bill Moseley never seemed to be at all bothered and he upset us once, for when the 'take cover' sounded and we did just that, all except Bill that is. The Anti-Personnel's were going off all around us, but Bill just went on with what he was doing, completely ignoring the attack. After the 'all clear' had sounded, we rounded up on him, calling him all sorts of names, depicting what sort of fathead he was for not taking cover like the rest of us. He just looked at us and said quietly 'I have no fear of these things, the Lord will protect me, I know because he told me.' Our flabber was absolutely garsted, we had no answer, so we let him alone. No one called him a useless Bible basher after that incident. I have never forgotten the incident and I have never forgotten what is meant by a 'true believer.'

One day, we found Freddie Soden in a terrible state, he was almost incoherent. After we had calmed him down, he blurted out the terrible news that 'Slash' and 'Tiffie' had gone missing. What a calamity, Freddie was inconsolable, his beloved rabbit had gone, he never wandered away and neither had 'Tiffie.' We had noticed a few times that some of the civilian workers had eyed our pets and mischievously rubbed their tummies with their hands, as to say 'they would make a nice meal.' We never said anything to Freddie, but we thought he already knew, we never expected one of the workers would sink so low, especially as we fed them as well as paying them for their labour.

On the brighter side, our entertainment officer told us he had arranged for our little dance band to play at the local hall, inviting some of the locals along to the dance. So off we went, after raking out our best blue and loading up our instruments on to a Bedford Lorry and then making our way down to Volkel town to play the dance. I cannot say we enjoyed the evening, for just as we were ready to start, a pretty girl came up to us and introduced herself; telling us in near perfect English that her name was 'Yet' – the Dutch version of our girls name Harriet. She went on to say that her uncle played the piano accordion and could he play in the band with us; she added this would be appreciated by the town's people. What could we say? Anything for a quiet life, at least that's what we thought.

When we played 'Lady be good' it sounded as if he was playing 'I'll take you home again Kathleen.' It was awful, he just sat there grunting and groaning on his Sqeezebox, but I think he was the only one who appreciated his efforts. I know we all wished he would go and play with the traffic. Toddy nearly choked when, after the dance had finished, 'Yet' asked us if her uncle would get paid like the rest of us. Needless to say, that was the last time we played in Volkel.

On day, when things were quiet, a couple of us decided that as our squadron had been 'stood down' we would venture to parts of the airfield where we had never been before. We stopped and had a chat with some of the RAF Regiment lads who were on their Ack Ack guns, well machine guns really. Their gun emplacement was well sandbagged up and looked quite cosy. Moving on, we came across what we thought was another disused gun emplacement, it was completely deserted, but curiosity got the better of us and we found a battered old doorway with rusty hinges, which creaked when we pushed the door open. Inside were piles of boxes and tins, but the state of the place suggested that whoever had been there, left in an almighty hurry.

We opened a few boxes and found the contents to be some sort of 'hard tac.' If you thought our biscuits were hard, you should have tried these. Streuth! They must have been made with 'Blue Circle' cement. We then opened a couple of tins and these contained what we assumed to be Jam. It was like stodgy red porridge, too thick to spoon out, so we had to cut it out in chunks. Although we tried putting it on about a quarter of an inch thick, it was still tasteless.

It dawned on us that we had found a food dump, we thought 'poor sods, if this is what they had to eat.' Compared to them, we lived like Lords. We went back to our dispersal and reported what we had found, but we never saw or heard any more about our find, so we assumed our superiors thought it was not worth bothering about.

One event that happened was beyond my wildest dreams. George Edwards told me while at breakfast, that a band was coming to give us a concert. This would be a novelty, for it was generally us who were entertaining other people. Anyway, later on that day as I was passing one of our makeshift hangars, which also served as a concert hall when the occasion demanded, as it had a disused flatbed trailer as a stage; I suddenly heard voices. I heard one chap say, they must have a left-handed guitarist here, for this guitar is strung up 'arse about face.' I announced indignantly that the guitar was mine, and what was he doing mucking around with it for?

He apologised and said his name was Sid Colin, had I heard of him? I gasped 'Sid Colin of the Squadronaires? He grinned and said 'you've got it.' I simply asked what was he doing here and he said that the 'Squads are playing here tonight.' He then introduced the chap standing beside him, 'this is our bagman Bill Nichols.' Without thinking I just queried 'The Boy Wonder? He groaned and said 'Won't I ever loose that bloody name? Billy had burst on the scene as a teenage musician on the London band circuit pre-war.

As we talked, other famous bandsman arrived, Tommy McQuater, Andy McDevitt, Ronnie Aldrich and Jock Cummings. Someone said 'What about a session? They asked me if I would care to sit in with them. I thoroughly enjoyed about an hour and eventually Jimmy Miller arrived and said 'Ok son, you can go back to the war now.' That night, my newly found friends treated us to the most memorable concert ever.

The next morning, as the 'Squads' were packing their gear into their lorry, Jimmy Miller came over to me and said 'Here you are Binkie, a souvenir.' It was a sheet of paper which said simply 'To Binkie from the Squadronaires,' it was signed by every member in the band. As he handed me the paper, we could hear explosions nearby, I remember Andy McDevitt saying are they bombs going off? I replied 'No they are guns.' He said 'Christ! Let's get out of here quick.' At that, the lorry disappeared in a bit of a hurry.

I experienced another of the scariest moments of my life, whilst I and my fellow comrade 'Bixie' were servicing one of our aircraft. Bixie had the cowling off, doing what we had to do, when we both heard the familiar sound of a Doodle Bug. To our horror, this thing was only twenty feet above the ground and was flying straight and level, straight at us. We were too petrified to move and watched it for what seemed an eternity, but in reality was only a couple of seconds, when it dived gently into the soft muddy ground. It exploded with a fairly quiet 'Boof' and that was it. We had survived, but neither of us was in any condition to carry on working, we were so shaken. Looking back, I think that was the last Doddle Bug I ever saw during the war, although at Volkel, we could see the V2s heading skywards at frequent intervals.

Then came the news we had all been waiting for. One of the 'erks' came rushing up to us and shouted 'the leave roster has gone up in the Admin. tent', you can imagine our reaction – LEAVE We had heard rumours that personnel who had been in Europe since the Normandy landings would be granted leave 'when the situation permitted', but now it was fact. When I made my way to the 'Admin' tent, I awaited my turn to see the list, and found my allotted time was (as I recall) 4th April 1945 for the period of 10 days. I was overjoyed, and as soon as I could, I wrote home to Win, and asked her if we could get married, when my leave came round. I also wrote home to Mum and Dad, telling them that I was coming home on leave, and that I had asked Win if we could get married, while I was home. A few days later (it seemed like an eternity) I had replies from Win and Mum. Apparently, the two sets of parents had got together when Win got a 24 hour pass, and the answer was yes!

I told all of my mates on 245 the good news and they were all happy for me, although no firm date was set. This happy period received a nasty jolt, when we again got the order 'Pack, ready to move'. This time was something a wee bit different for we were going into 'Das Reich'. What a turn up for the book – in 1940 we were expecting Hitler and his gang to invade our tiny Island – 'Der Fuehrer' had already promised his people that he would lead his Army 'Up Whitehall' but now the boot was well and truly on the other foot, for it was us doing the invading, and in style!

We drove through heavily wooded areas, and wondered if this was the famous Black Forest. Eventually, we came out into the open country, and soon found our latest 'home'. I think the name of the place was Celle (apparently it was somewhere near Osnabruck). We were quite 'chuffed' to think that we would be operating against the Germans in their own back yard, or should I say 'from their own back yard'. Somehow, it seemed a bit of a let-down as although we were continually on 'ops' nothing exciting seemed to be happening, whether we had done something to upset Jerry, but we weren't bombed, strafed or shelled, in fact it reminded me of one of Stanley Holloway's monologues, when he was disappointed with Blackpool by declaring 'They didn't think much of the Ocean, - the waves they were fiddling and small, there were no wrecks and nobody drowned, in fact – nothing to laugh at, at all' that's how it seemed now, something of an anti-climax.

Before I knew it April arrived, and I was getting all 'geared up' for my impending leave. Came April 4th and as I was packing my 'small kit' I got the news I was dreading – 'Sorry Binkie, but the sailings are delayed for 24 hours because of rough seas'. This was a hell of a shock, for I was due to get married on the 7th, and if I didn't sail on the next day, I would not be home in time for my own wedding. I was on tenterhooks all day and night, and I was a bag of nerves until I was told 'It's alright Binkie, the lorry leaves at 10 o'clock, be on it.'

I barely had time to say my farewells, when Lindesey came up and said that the adjutant wanted to see me. Oh corks or something like that I thought – what now? I dashed round to Tommy Thompson's tent (he was the adjutant) and he met me with a broad grin, and said the lads have had a whip round and, this is for you. He gave me an envelope with some money in it, and then said to me 'and this is for you from me' and handed me a bottle of Champagne.

I boarded the lorry for the first stage of my journey home, and I took Win's latest letter from my pocket, to make sure I was not dreaming. It was all there, the date had been set (April 7th), the chapel was booked, the minister had agreed to officiate, and the invitations were going out. Win was delighted to tell me that her sister's wedding dress fitted her, and I thought 'good old Maisie'. My sister Fay and Win's cousin Pearl were to be bridesmaids, and my cousin Henry was to be best man. My mother had sorted out a Wedding ring, so all I had to do now was to turn up at the right place at the right time. The lorry arrived at some sort of Belgian Army Barracks, and after a brief stay, we entrained to Calais. As luck would have it, there were no more delays as things were back to normal in the English Channel.

It was a glorious day, and sailing across the Channel was just like a trip on the old 'Royal Eagle' which plied her way to Clacton or Margate before the war. Mid- morning and the shout went up 'The White Cliffs of Dover'. We looked, and there they were, just as we knew they would look. I have never seen so many men openly weeping, because this was their home – the most wonderful place in the world to the returning troops.

It was a never to be again experience, when we walked down the gangplank and set foot in dear old England once more. I could not help thinking that this was something the Germans could not do, in spite of their might and power. We were quickly directed on to the trains, passing through cheering crowds - even the Redcaps looked happy for us – we were home, if only for a few days.

We pulled into Charing Cross station, and being on familiar ground, I dashed round to the Tube – the dear old District Line to Mark Lane as it was called then (now it is Tower Hill), round the corner to Seething Lane, up the steps I knew so well and on to Fenchurch Street Station. It was so quiet, not like the crowds greeting us at Charing Cross. No matter, I settled for Fenchurch Street for it was there that the train took me to Grays.

As I left Grays station, and looked down the high street, I stopped and looked. Nothing had changed, Woolworths and Marks and Spencer's were there, so was Westwoods the High class gents outfitters, and there was the dear old Empire – the old Victoria Theatre turned cinema, where I used to go on a Saturday morning for the 'three ha'penny rush' to see Tom Mix, Ken Maynard, Bill Boyd and other cowboys. Down to the Queens Arms, a brief stop at the war memorial, then five minutes-walk to Hathaway Road, and I was home. I stopped at the front gate and looked round, there was no one about; not even a neighbour, so I put my key in the front door, and there was Mum, smiling with tears in her eyes and a big hug. 'What can I get you, son?' was all she said, so I just said 'a nice cup of tea' and as an afterthought – a nice hot bath – I haven't had once since last June.

After a good soaking, I told mum that I was going to meet Dad from work. I walked into Grays and waited for his bus to come in. As he got off the bus I said 'Hi, Pop' as I always did, and he said something like 'You got home alright then Son, had a good trip?' After tea, I said I was off to see Win, and caught the bus into Aveley, where she lived. I rung her front door bell, the door opened, and there she was radiant, smiling, almost in tears. We just fell into each other's arms for a few moments before we went into the sitting room to meet the rest of her family. I was greeted like a long lost son, and I can remember saying to Maisie – 'I couldn't get to your wedding Maisie, but you can come to mine, tomorrow'.

The evening passed quickly, and it was time for me to go home, so I said my 'good-nights' to Win's family and she walked with me to the bus top. As I boarded the bus and stood at the rear platform, I realised that I had never really proposed to Win, and as the bus pulled away, I called out 'Win… will you marry me?' She called out 'Yes' so I waved to her and sat on the nearest seat. The look the conductor gave me was worth seeing, and I bet he told all of his mates back at the Garage about the weird airman he had on his bus.

The next morning, everyone at home was dashing about, getting in each other's way, doing something that someone else had already done, when Mum asked me to pop round to the florists and pick up the flowers. To be honest I was glad to get out of the way. My sister-in-law's young sister Jean, who I stayed with at Beeleigh two years before volunteered to help me, so we walked into Grays and picked up the flowers. It was a good job Jean came with me, for I could never have managed on my own.

After a mid-morning snack, all my family made their way over to Aveley, leaving me to have a last minute bath, before Henry came to escort me to the church. As all the old time comedians used to say 'A funny thing happened to me on the way here tonight' – a funny thing happened to me on the way to the church....The bus arrived at Aveley, and as we had plenty of time, I suggested to Henry that it would be a good idea to have a quick drink in the 'Prince Albert'. This we did and made our way to the church that I knew was only fifty yards away. Funny...when we got to the church, there was no one there. I tried the door, and found it was locked. Henry was quick to work it out, for he said 'We must be at the wrong church'. I answered 'But there isn't another church in Aveley', panic stations.

We walked back to the church gates, and I asked a passing woman, 'Is there another church in Aveley besides this one?' She said that there wasn't. In desperation I said 'There must be, for I am getting married in about ten minute's time'. She thought for a few moments and said thoughtfully 'Well, there is the chapel halfway up the high street, why don't you try there'. Henry and I got our 'skates on' and dashed up the high street, and sure enough we could see a crowd of people waving their arms and shouting 'Come on, hurry up'.

We arrived at the chapel, and demanded to know why no one had thought to tell me, we were getting married in the chapel and not in church; after all I was only the flipping bridegroom wasn't I. However, all went well after that. I felt so sorry for Win, what must she have been thinking, sitting in the Ante-Room, wondering if I was going to turn up. As it happened when her Dad led her up the aisle, she was so composed and when she held my hand, I thought she was going to break my fingers, - she held them so tight.

After the ceremony, we all made our way up to the village hall for photographs, and the reception, which went off surprisingly well. In the evening, we had dancing and then Win and I had the 'first Waltz', I realised that this was the first time we had ever danced together. At this stage, I realised also, that Win had invited a few of her WAAF friends from High Wycombe and got to know them, and I must admit I was pleased to know that Win had made friends with such nice girls. All too soon, our leave was up, the time had simply flown by. Win came down to Grays with me, while I said my farewells to my family, and then walked up to the station to Fenchurch Street. We hugged and kissed on the platform, until the train came in. I shall never forget seeing her on the platform waving, until she was out of sight. I have never felt so alone in my life, and all the time I could hear her voice over and over again saying, 'Please, come home safely to me.'

CHAPTER 9
Das Reich & England, Home & Beauty

At Charing Cross, the station was heaving with soldiers and airmen waiting for their trains to take them to Dover. I don't remember anything about the journey to Dover, all I could think about was my Win, and when I would see her again. At Dover, we were marched down to the harbour, where our ship was waiting to take us back to war. Once on board, I could hear the ship's radio playing, and I could hear Win singing our favourite song 'Someday I'll see you again, don't know where, don't know when,' it was too much for me and I sobbed like a four year old. I don't remember much about the journey back to our airstrip, I was so miserable, but once I was with my friends I felt a lot better – they all wanted to know how the wedding went, and thought it was quite funny when I told them about the incident when I went to the wrong church.

There was an air of 'it will soon be over now' and although operations carried on as usual, it was nowhere as hectic as it had been for the last few months, but there was one memorable day when our troops crossed the River Rhine. I think it was somewhere around midday, when we heard the sound of aero engines, and once again we saw the spectacle of an air armada heading eastwards towards the heart of Germany. There were the usual assortment of Lancasters, Halifaxes, and Dakotas towing Gliders, and we all said our silent prayers for our Paratroopers, and we rightly guessed that this was the assault on the River Rhine. On the return journey, many of the 'four engine jobs' flew so low, that we could actually see the nose and rear gunners waving to us as they flew over our airfield. I could somehow picture the pilots saying on the intercom something like 'Captain to all crew, if you look down now, you will see our own aircraft on a captured airfield.'

It was wonderful to see the aircrews waving like mad as they made their way homewards. Needless to say, all us 'erks' waved and danced about in return. The crossing was confirmed on the Forces programme on the radio, when they announced that the River Rhine had been crossed by the airborne and seaborne forces. Yes, even the navy had been involved, carrying our troops over in their tiny craft, a truly wonderful combined operations attack involving all three services. We knew then, that it was only a matter of time before the Germans capitulated. Our joy was dented however, when some of our officers made a journey by road to the nearby Concentration

Camp, 'Belsen.' They returned shocked, dazed, they just could not believe what they had seen. It seemed they could not comprehend that anyone could treat fellow humans like the Germans treated the Jews. One of the officers had taken a camera with him and had taken photos of conditions in Belsen. He handed his camera to Johnny Johnson, the corporal in charge of the Photographic Section and asked him to develop and print his film.

I had always been pally with the photo bods, Johnny Johnson and Frank Hegarty in particular, and   I happened to be around when the film was developed so I was shown the photos, they were of rotting corpses, piled high, survivors like living skeletons dressed in filthy clothes were there to be seen, pictures of the ovens where the victims were incinerated and proved that bestiality was rife in the 'herronvolk.' Any sympathy I had for the German troops who were subjected to the bombing of Caen and Villers Bocarge some months earlier, disappeared and I could only think that these so called people, should be wiped off the face of the earth. Where were the so called 'good Germans? Surely the local inhabitants knew what was going on, and remember there were dozens of these Concentration Camps, so the German population must have known what was going on.

It was then that we realised what the funny smell was, that hung around. A dirty sickly smell that you could not identify; so now we knew, it was the stench from Belsen which was miles away. Goodness knows what it was like inside the camp.

In my mind's eye, I can still see the face of the camp kommondant known as 'the beast of Belsen' which was published in the newspapers a few days later.

It was now the month of May and we hoped that any day now the war would be over. Sure enough on 8th May 1945, we heard on the radio the news we had been waiting for. Winston Churchill announced to the world that the German Forces had unconditionally surrendered to Field Marshal Bernard Montgomery and the war was at an end.

Everyone was jubilant and we all talked about getting back home, back to our loved ones, our own homes and back to our old jobs. Then some bright spark spoilt it all, when he reminded us that there was still another war going on in the Pacific and we would probably be sent out there, now that Jerry had packed it in. That was something we did not relish, then someone came up with the suggestion that by the time we had got reorganised, with the time it would take to get out there, it could possibly be at and end. With that thought, things didn't seem too bad, we would just have to wait and see, besides, there would have to be some sort of army of occupation. On top of that, we were reminded that there were still some fanatical Germans who would defy the armistice and carry on fighting. As it happened, this is exactly what did happen, although where we were there was only isolated groups of resistance, and these we got to know as 'Werewolves.'

At this point I must mention our Corporal Redcap 'Paddy' Greer. He was I suppose one of the bravest or stupidest men I have ever met. He went into the adjacent woods with his Alsation on what he called 'Security Patrols' every day for weeks; he would set off and come back with two, three or even more Germans as his prisoners. If ever a man deserved a decoration, it was 'Paddy,' but whether he did or not, I do not know.

No rest for the wicked goes the old saying, and sure enough we got orders to pack up and get ready to move. We thought those days were gone, but no, we were off again. This time the journey was so very different from any other that we had made. We went through town after town, or rather what was left of them. I shall never forget the devastation I saw as we passed through Hamburg, the whole city and I mean whole city was just one scene of utter and complete ruin. We all knew that Hamburg had received a lot of hammer, for the BBC gave out so many times 'This is the BBC News and this is Alva Liddell reading it.

Hamburg was again attacked last night by a strong force of bombers.' We had heard it so many times, but no way could we contemplate the scale of the devastation we now witnessed. I can remember one of my mates saying 'Bomber Harris was right when he said that Jerry had started it, now we shall finish it.'

We eventually arrived at our new home and it also turned out to be our last for 121 Wing. We were almost on the Danish border at a place called Schleswig Holstein.

It was a very large aerodrome and as we explored the place, we found so many different and interesting aircraft besides Junkers Ju88s and Heinkel 111s. There was also a Messerschmitt 262, the first jet aircraft ever used in aerial warfare. The biggest surprise however, came when we found a camouflaged hangar on the edge of the airfield, apart from the camouflage; it was also hidden by overhanging trees. In this hangar was a four-engine bomber! As far as I know, no-one has ever mentioned that the Germans had a four engine machine, but there it was as large as life, or rather as large as a Lancaster or Halifax. I could not tell you the make of the monster, no-one could tell me, but it was a guess that it was a Heinkel, for they were responsible for the Luftwaffe's main bomber during the whole war. *

This was what we called a 'shaky do! Had Jerry introduced this aircraft a couple of years earlier, goodness knows what impact it would have made to the outcome of the war. I can only assume, as Hitler and his cohorts did, the war was only going to last a year or two, then his armada of twin engine bombers would have sufficed. This train of thought would have been correct if it were not for the boys of Fighter Command in 1940, when the 'Few' sorted out the Luftwaffe during the Battle of Britain.

We also discovered a couple of Dornier 17s, a twin-engine civil airliner and a Fiesler Storch, the German equivalent of our Westland Lysander, affectionately known as the 'Lizzie.' It was this particular 'Storch' that gave us a bit of a fright, when one of our pilots decided he would show us how to fly this machine. He took off, executed a couple of circuits; then he decided to 'beat up' our dispersal. He came in at zero feet, when oops-a- daisy his wheels touched the ground, so did his wings and so did the fuselage, or rather what was left of it. After the dust had settled, we ran to see if the pilot was OK. As it happened, he came staggering away from what looked like a heap of matches, muttering something like 'that was a bloody silly thing to do.' Nobody said anything, but we all agreed with him, for he could have so easily killed himself in an idiotic prank.

As far as the civil aircraft was concerned, our commanding officer Squadron Leader Schweiberg hit on the idea of taking some of us 'erks' on a short flight around Schleswig and the surrounding countryside. He also flew over the seaplane base at Schleswig; where there was about a dozen Arado seaplanes riding at anchor. After the flight, we asked him what it was like to fly a twin-engine job; he told us quite simply that before the war, he was a pilot for Swiss Air. It did seem a bit odd, an experienced airline pilot flying fighter aircraft, but as the old saying goes, 'worse things happen at sea.'

It was at Schleswig that I had the most eerie experience of my life. Now that the war was finally over, we were allowed to go into the town, but it was emphasized, we were not allowed to fraternise with the locals. One day I decided to have a look at the town and perhaps browse around the shops. There was not much to see and I was about to turn around and make my way back to the airfield, when something made me stop. The hair on my neck stood up, and I was frightened for I had the feeling that I had been here before. This was out of the question for until I had joined the RAF, I had never been any further than Ramsgate in Kent, but here I was in north-east Germany with this strange feeling. I knew that there was a shop that sold bric-a-brac and memorabilia round the next corner.

Curiosity made me carry on walking and turning the corner, was a shop with ornaments and military items, badges of rank, chevrons, various items of headgear, water bottles etc. How did I know that such a shop existed in a place I had never heard of, let alone visited before? Then the thought struck me, could it be that I had been here before? Not in this life that's for sure, but in a previous life. I had heard of reincarnation and what it meant, but I never believed in it. But what other explanation was there? I returned to the airfield, thoroughly shaken and baffled. Needless to say, I never visited the town again.

Our pilots were not allowed to get 'stale' so they did quite a lot of formation flying. Our aircraft were also 'spruced up' all spick and span, then somebody had the bright idea of painting the spinners. All through the war years, our aircraft always had cream coloured spinners, but now for some reason each squadron had their own coloured spinners; we on 245 had red, whilst 174, 175 and 184 had blue, green and yellow ones. We were told it would help identify our own squadrons. To us it was just plain daft, as we could already identify our squadrons by the code lettering on the side of the fuselages, ours being MR. Anyway as long as it made someone happy, we could not have cared less. The one consolation was to see our aircraft fly over the airfield in tight formation. It was great, for it could not be easy for the pilots to keep a tight 'Vic' at nearly 400 mph. Bully for them.

It was in August 1945, we were sitting in our crew-room and outside it was pelting with rain; we were listening to the radio, when suddenly the programme was interrupted for an important announcement. This was to say that a nuclear bomb had been delivered on the Japanese city of Hiroshima and that the city had been completely obliterated. There was no cheering or anything, but someone said quietly 'What the hell is a nuclear bomb? When it was explained to us, and then told that the Germans had also been working on the same type of bomb, it made us realise how important it was for us to end the war in Europe quickly.

A couple of days later, another announcement told us that the Americans had dropped another nuclear bomb, this time on Nagasaki. We received this news with mixed feelings, to kill people in their hundreds of thousands wasn't war, but wholesale slaughter. One of the intelligence officers gave us a short chat about this, it was not a lecture, just an informal update of the pros and cons. Briefly it boiled down to two options, we either bombed the Japanese with a few nuclear bombs on say, Tokyo and Yokohama or we the Allies would have horrendous casualties, knowing that the Japanese have a complete disregard of loss of life and consider it an honour to die for their Emperor. They would fight every inch to save their country, whatever the cost. I heard one 'erk' say 'but there are millions of the little bastards, how would we be able to cope with all of them? The officer said 'Nuclear bombing would cost hundreds of thousands of Japanese lives, but would save millions of Allied ones, not just Americans, but Britons, Australian, Indians and other nationalities as well.'

This was food for thought, coming to the conclusion that D-Day was a picnic compared to an invasion of Japan. In 1944 after the invasion, we thought of the hell on the Normandy beaches, we said 'Please God, let this never happen again 'We couldn't let it happen again, we had to use those bombs if need be.' As it happened and I like to think it was divine intervention, the Japanese agreed to an unconditional surrender to the Allies. Just as Field Marshal Montgomery accepted the surrender of the Germans, General McArthur accepted the Japanese surrender on behalf of the Allied forces. So that was it then, no more fighting and we would finally be allowed to go home, thank God.

It was shortly after that our commanding officer, Group Captain Morice called us all on parade and announced that No.121 Wing had been granted seven days leave, everyone! This was greeted with cheering, but he continued by saying that unfortunately, only one squadron could go at a time, so the leave order would be by ballot, it was just our luck that 245 Squadron would be the last in the pecking order. The following week, all the bods on 174 Squadron packed their 'small kit' and whisked off to Flensburg for seven days. They returned after their leave loaded with cameras, binoculars watches etc, which they had procured by barter. The same thing happened to the next lot to go to Flensburg, by now we were hoarding our cigarettes and chocolates like squirrels, so that we would be prepared when it was our turn to go, hoping fervently that all the 'goodies' hadn't gone by then.

We were all minding our own business on the dispersal on a bright sunny day, when the Tannoy blared out 'All 245 Squadron personnel to report to the Mess Hangar immediately.' This was what we were waiting for, our turn to go on leave to Flensburg, but we were mistaken, for when we were all assembled in the hangar, Group Captain Morice stood on a chair and said 'Today, I received notification that 121 Wing is to be disbanded and that all personnel are to be repatriated. This comes into immediate effect.' He went on to say that as 245 Squadron would be the first to leave for England, we were to return to our quarters and pack our kit, ready to move tomorrow morning. He dismissed the parade, and you could not see our backsides for dust. Before I packed my kit however, I dashed off a few lines to Win and to my mother, to say that I should be back in the UK in a couple of days.

In the morning, we said our farewells to our pals and climbed on to the lorries which took us to the railway station. When the train came into the station, we took one look at it and thought 'Blimey! The thing must have come out of the Ark. It was so old and the carriage looked like something that Stephenson's 'Rocket' cast off. When we opened the carriage doors, we found wooden seats and the windows boarded up. After reflection, we came to the conclusion that it was our own fault; after all, it was Bomber Command who had knocked the hell bells out of the German Railway system for the last few years. Still beggars can't be choosers and we were on our way home.

Our train chugged its way through Germany, through devastated towns, lovely countryside and at one stage, as the line ran alongside a river, which could have been the Rhine, we saw a bridge or rather what was left of it, most of which had capsized into the river. I wondered at the time if it was the now famous Bridge at Ramagen. Whatever it was, it was in a very sorry state and I couldn't help wondering, how many poor souls had died; the Germans who had died defending it and the Americans who died attempting to take the bridge intact.

We eventually stopped at a small town, where we were allowed to stretch our legs, and have a cup of tea and a sandwich. Would you be surprised, Corned Beef, at least it was not a 'curly' sandwich that we used to get at the tea rooms on British Railway stations.

Back on the train for the next leg home and by now the sun was making the carriages hot and stifling, for as I had previously mentioned, the windows had been boarded up. By mid-afternoon it had got unbearably hot, one of the erks said 'I've had enough of this' and got up from his seat, grabbed his rifle and smashed the wood in the windows, so that we could get some fresh air. That was fine for the time being, that is! As evening came, the weather changed and soon it was pelting with rain. It so happened that the bod who had smashed the wooden window was sitting in the corner seat, consequently, he got ever so slightly wet. It didn't do much to help him when we laughed at his plight. By the time it was dark it got quite cold and we were thankful that we had our greatcoats to put on.

We eventually reached our destination, it turned out to be a small seaside town called Blankenberg; we were shuttled off to a small hotel, where we would stay for a day or two. It was nice to have a bed to crawl into after roughing it for so long.

After a good night's sleep, we had the luxury of having a breakfast without having to line up with a mess tin, knife, fork and spoon. The day was ours to do with as we pleased, and I spent most of the day resting on the beautiful sandy beach.

After tea that evening, we were told that we would be on the move again in the morning, so it would be wise to have an early night. We needed no second telling for we realised that the past twelve months was taking its toll, we were all very tired and badly needed a good rest.

Came the morning and it was back aboard the lorries to goodness knows where. It did not seem very long before we could see cranes and gantries, so we knew then that we had arrived at our embarking point. When we saw the direction sign with Ostend greeting us, we knew we would soon be aboard a ship on our way back to dear old England. As we climbed off the lorries and lined up for embarkation, we were addressed by a nasty looking Redcap with three stripes, who told us with great relish that we could only go aboard with what we could carry. There would be no going back for what we could not carry. Anything that could not be carried would be confiscated. Someone at the back shouted out 'you mean nicked, you lousy bleeder.'

Anyway some of the erks who had excess gear, hit on the idea of working in twos, by laying their rifles side by side and piling their kit and other items on top, carrying their rifles like a stretcher, walking up the gangplank one behind the other – simple!

Having overcome this little obstacle, we set sail for home. As soon as we were out of the harbour, the Tannoy announced that it was illegal to take firearms into our country and anyone caught carrying a firearm, even though it was a souvenir, would be charged and possibly court-marshalled for the offence. I don't mind telling you that there were quite a lot of little splashes in the North Sea on the way home!

As our ship ploughed its way across the sea, it suddenly dawned on me that we were quite alone. Not another ship to be seen anywhere and it made me think and wonder how men coped when they were alone in a dinghy, as many an airman was, when shot down and baled out into the sea, or the survivors of a ship that had been torpedoed and were in a life raft perhaps for days on end; only those who survived this ordeal could answer this.

We eventually arrived back in dear old England and silently thanked God for our safe return. We were directed to our train and to be honest, I was so tired that I could not remember much about the train journey, for I slept most of the time.

When the train reached its destination, we were ushered on to waiting vehicles and driven to our last RAF station of the war. What a shock we had, for the first thing we saw was a couple of SPs on the gate immaculately dressed, shiny boots and white covers on their caps. The stones round the guard room were painted white, the buildings, yes real buildings, looked as though they were dusted and polished every day. Where the hell were we? It turned out to be Dunsfold in Surrey. Apparently it was in the 'Stockbroker Belt' and we were told it was the 'nicest County in England'. We were quite 'chuffed' at that, after being among the war torn towns and villages in Europe.

We were allocated to our billets, which had real beds, curtains at the windows, and polished wooden floors. We thought we were in heaven. We had a rude awakening however, when we decided to go over to the NAAFI for when we walked in, we looked and felt out of place among the airmen and WAAF's who all looked as though they had just come out of the tailors shop, while we were still in our Battle Dress Blouses. It made matters worse when one WAAF said rather loudly 'who are these scruffy lot? You would think they would have the decency to put their best uniforms on'.

Quite out of character, I walked over to the table where this offensive WAAF sat with her friends, and said something like 'Excuse me Miss, but these are our best uniforms, and for the past year we have been in Europe, sleeping in tents and ditches. We have been

114

bombed, shelled, strafed and working up to sixteen hours a day. I'm very sorry, but under these conditions we didn't have clothing parades every week, and our clothes laundered for us, there were not any shops to get metal polish or Cherry Blossom for our Boots. In any case most of us have literally had to live in our Gum Boots, so we had no use for them anyway.'

As I turned away, as an afterthought, I pointed to my campaign medal ribbons and said 'and we didn't get these sitting in cosy Surrey and taking the mickey out of people who had been fighting for their safety.' One airman sitting nearby got up to protest, and Taffy Jones an ex coal miner who weighed something like sixteen stones, simply said to him 'forget it chum, we are all trained in unarmed combat, and wouldn't like to spoil your pretty uniform.' Needless to say, the airman sat down again.

So this was our welcome back to England, what a load of snobs we found ourselves with. As I still felt angry with the WAAF who was so snooty, I thought 'she isn't a real WAAF, not like the girls I worked with at Martlesham, - Joyce, Connie, Barbara, Ursula, Chrissie and the others, but then again, these girls were on an operational station. Then I thought of my Win, she was a WAAF and so were her friends at High Wycombe, Sheila, Daisy and Pat.

The following day was a 'free' day, which meant that we could do as we wished, so I hit on the idea of going to see Win. I forget which railway station I went to, but I made enquiries as to how I could get to High Wycombe. Taking their advice, I took a train to Marylebone, where I could get a train to High Wycombe. It was a beautiful day and I enjoyed the journey, but I must say that I was very apprehensive as to how I could find out how I could get to Win.

This was when fate took a hand, for when I came out of the station, and looked around I could see literally hundreds of airmen and WAAF's walking about, some in ones and twos, some in small groups, and then for some unknown reason, I saw a WAAF walking on her own, and I approached her and said 'Excuse me, but could you tell me how I get to Bomber Command Headquarters, for I have just come home from Germany, and I want to see my wife.' So she said that there was a liberty wagon going there in a few minutes and as she was making her way to it, she would take me. She asked me what my wife did in the WAAF's and I told her that Win was a Batwoman. She said that she knew a few Batwomen and what was her name? I replied 'Win Bayford, but her name before we married was Win Beard'. Her face lit up, and she said 'Oh, I know Win well, and I can take you straight to the house where she works'. This, she did and opened the door and called out, 'Win, are you there, for there is someone to see you.' Moments later, we were in each other's arms, a moment I shall never, ever forget.

We spent a couple of hours together, strolling through the grounds surrounding the Headquarters before I had to return to Dunsfold. Before I left however, I asked Win if she would make enquiries regarding her discharge from the WAAF (as she was entitled to do now that I was back in England). I also told her that I would be having some disembarkation leave, could she get leave at the same time? This, she did, and we were on leave together, this time, not having to worry about going back into action. This was it – the end of my war, not a spectacular war, but an eventful one, having been shot at, shelled, strafed and bombed. I had witnessed massed air raids, unimaginable destruction, refugees, thousands of German prisoners, taken part in the world's biggest seaborne invasion, made so many friends, had a thousand memories, some good, some bad, and finally marrying the girl I loved, but it was my war – just an ordinary war – an erks war.

POSTSCRIPT

Ron Bayford was born at the family home, 133 Argent Street in Grays, Essex on 19th August 1922, next to the Seabrooke Brewery. He attended the Arthur Street Junior Comprehensive School and finished his education at the Park Senior School.

Ron was just thirteen and half years old, when he joined his first employment at Drums Limited in Thames Road, Grays. In 1938, he gained employment at the Thames Board Mills located at Purfleet. Here he became a registered clerk and board inspector.

After the war, Ron and Win returned to civilian life, although this was very hard and rationing continued for many years to come. Ron managed to return to his old job with the Thames Board Mills and became a Quality Controller. He remained with the firm until his retirement in 1978.

They had one son named Peter and a daughter, Janet. They have four grandchildren and three great grandchildren. Sadly Win passed away in October 2008.

Ron is still a staunch supporter of the church and has given his time and worked at the famous St. Clements' Church in West Thurrock.

Ron's favourite hobby is Bowls. He first became interested in 1946 and still plays today. He was elected officer of the Thurrock District Bowls Association and has served eight years as President.

Still very active, now in his 90th year, Ron gives as much time as he can, helping out other local people.

APPPENDIX A
Ron Bayford's Service Movements UK/Europe 1940-1945

Cardington	December 1940	Attested
Blackpool	February 1941	Training
Wilmslow	February 1941	Training
Skegness	February 1941	Passing out
Melksham	March 1941	12 School .Tech Training
Hawkinge	May 1941	91 Sqdn
Lympne	February 1942	91 Sqdn
Stapleford Tawney	May 1942	3203 SC
HMS Dundonald	May 1942	3203 SC
Inverary	May 1942	3203 SC
Lympne	May 1942	3203 SC
Martlesham	June 1942	Detached to SHQ
Lympne	December 1942	91 Sqdn
Hawkinge	January 1943	91 Sqdn
Wrexham	February 1943	121 Wing 2nd TAF
Middle Wallop	March 1943	19 Sqdn
		247 Sqdn
		182 Sqdn
Membury	March 1943	182 Sqdn
Middle Wallop	March 1943	182 Sqdn
Fairlop	April 1943	247 Sqdn
Selsey	April 1943	65 Sqdn
Lydd	May 1943	174 Sqdn
Attlebridge	September 1943	174 Sqdn
Westhampnett	October 1943	245 Sqdn
Holmsley South	March 1944	"
Horsham	May 1944	"
Eastchurch	May 1944	"
Holmsley South	May 1944	245 Sqdn
Oldsarum	June 1944	"
Fareham	June 1944	"
Gosport	6th June 1944 D-Day	"
Normandy	D-Day+6	"

Camilly Sur Mur		"
St Croix		"
Camilly Sur Mur		"
St Andre	July	"
Beauvais		"
Douai	August	"
Antwerp	September	"
Volkel	October/November	"
Celle	February 1945	"
Scheswig	May	"

The reason for us to be allocated to different squadrons was for us to familiarise ourselves with different aircraft for example Spitfires, Hurricanes, Typhoons and Tempests etc.

APPENDIX B

The Formation and Training of the Servicing Commando Units

The initial idea of the Servicing Commando Units began when it was decided by the tactical planners of the armed services that any invasion force in the future that gained a foothold on enemy held Europe, would need a mobile force of experienced tradesmen to service aircraft, once the enemy airfields had been captured by the advancing Allied Armies. The role of the units would be to keep a constant supply of the necessities for keeping the aircraft in combat readiness. This would mean large quantities of aviation fuel, oil, glycol coolant, spare parts and ammunition and of course food, water and basic accommodation.

On 31st January 1942, the Director of Organisation at the Air Ministry gave instructions that the formation of three Servicing Commando Units could go ahead, although this was met by both the Army and the RAF with an equal share of scepticism. One person who clearly championed the idea of forming these new tactical units was the chief of the Combined Operations at this time, Commodore Louis Mountbatten.

Orders were sent to RAF Training Command to form three volunteer SCUs and notices began to appear on Station Standing Orders asking for officers and men of various trades to volunteer for dangerous tasks that were unspecified.

The role of the units was detailed as follows:

The object of these units will be the occupation of advanced landing grounds as soon as they are captured by the army.

The Commando units would be put ashore by landing craft, complete with their own transport and equipment and make their way to the captured airfield or landing strip. Once set up, the fighter squadrons would fly in and be serviced by the Commando units. RAF Fighter Command would be responsible for the deployment of the SCUs. Each SCU would be trained to service front-line aircraft and keep them operational top support the advancing troops on the ground. As the battle moved forward, each SCU would pack up and move as another airfield was taken.

Each unit would comprise of two officers and 148 other ranks. The commanding officer, usually the rank of squadron leader would be a technical officer; his second in command would be an administration officer. Each unit was divided into Flights, three technical and one HQ Flight, each commanded by a flight sergeant. Each Flight was divided into four sections, with a corporal in charge.

Transportation for each unit consisted of fifteen 3-ton trucks, one motor-cycle and a jeep for the commanding officer. A minimum of equipment was only carried in the trucks and would be evenly distributed to minimise the effect of damage to the vehicles.

The men who enrolled for the SCUs would undertake rigorous training; this included unarmed combat, forced marches, swimming, map reading and bayonet practice. Every man had to be able to drive and be capable of maintaining a vehicle and instruction on how to waterproof the vehicle which might take part in the invasion, if off-loaded into deep water off the beach-head.

Those who passed the first stage of training were then sent north to Scotland, to Inverary on Loch Fyne. Here was situated the Inverary Combined Services Training Centre which was manned by instructors of all the three armed services. The SCUs were then put aboard the *HMT Etterick*, a Royal Navy Landing Ship, to undertake instruction on how to load and disembark vehicles, mobile equipment and the use of scrabbling nets, slung over the ships side. The training was carried out in both day and night-time conditions.

Landing exercises were carried out under various conditions. A final practice was carried out by the SCUs under training with a landing using live ammunition and smoke. After two-weeks of training, the units were put to sea in a landing craft, whatever the weather conditions would throw up, to undertake a final practice landing on the beaches at Troon, Ayrshire.

Those units who passed through were then sent to undergo training on various aircraft currently operational with the Royal Air Force and the United States Army Air Force. This course was completed with instruction on anti-aircraft weapons and aircraft recognition.

In all, fifteen Servicing Commando Units were formed in the United Kingdom and the Middle East. During the summer of 1943, three smaller units had also been formed in India to undertake operations in Burma.

APPENDIX C

A letter from Louis Mountbatten, Commodore Combined Operations regarding formation of RAF Servicing Commandos

War Cabinet Annexe,
1a Richmond Terrace,
Whitehall SW1

22nd January 1942

To: Air Ministry D.C.O
Copy to Air Ministry (D.D.T. (Combined Operations)
D.S. Ops
D.B. Ops
D.S.C
C. in C. Fighter Command

Formation of RAF Servicing Commandos
for use in Combined Operations

1. In most combined operations the capture as soon as possible of an enemy aerodrome will be essential in order to allow our fighter, tactical reconnaissance and possibly bomber support aircraft to operate at maximum efficiency.
2. During the early stages it is probable that the use of a captured aerodrome would be limited to refuelling, rearming, flight maintenance, minor repairs and the minimum essential communications.
3. It is suggested that special servicing units should be established with the necessary ground personnel to undertake these duties on the basis of say one servicing unit to look after three squadrons.
4. This matter has already been discussed by Air Commodore Walker with the Director of Fighter Operations who put forward a minute to the Deputy Chief of Air Staff on 15th January 1942, outlining the various stages in the process of a

combined operation as far as fighter squadrons are concerned and recommending the formation of a special servicing unit of this nature.

5. For easy reference the recommendations put forward to D.S.A.S are reproduced below.

(a) Form RAF Servicing Commandos with their equipment, and make them an essential part of the various fighter groups.

(b) Train these Commandos in their specific duties under the control of groups. In this way they will achieve cohesion and RAF esprit de corps.

(c) As soon as we have some Commandos trained in their air duties, they should be sent in turn to the Combined Training Centre where they would go through a thorough training in their Commando duties.

(d) Each fighter group, whose Commandos were under training at the Combined Training Centre, would then send fighter squadrons in rotation to be trained in combined operations with the other services.

6. Air Commodore Walker has discussed these proposals with the A.O.C Fighter Command, who expressed his approval of the scheme in principle.

7. If and when such units are formed, I suggest that on completion of their air duties training, they should be sent to the Combined Training Centre at Auchengate for periods of extensive training in combined operations with the Expeditionary Force. This training would include being put ashore over the beaches and taking part in exercises in which they would be employed at the Combined Operations aerodrome in servicing operational squadrons under war conditions.

8. After training it is hoped that a number of these servicing Commandos would be definitely held in reserve to accompany the Expeditionary Force should they be required.

Louis Mountbatten (Commodore Combined Operations)

APPENDIX D

Some of the distinguished fighter pilots who served with
No. 91 'Nigeria' Squadron during my service with them

Wing Commander/Lieutenant Colonel Jean-Francois Demozay (Moses) DSO, DFC*

Demozay was born in Nantes on 21st March 1916 and was called up for military service in 1938, but was invalided out only a month later. He fortunately became a civil pilot and at the outbreak of war he offered his services, but was accepted for non-combatant duties. He was seconded to the RAF during the Battle of France as an interpreter joining No. 1 Squadron. During the retreat from France by the Royal Air Force, he was unable to accompany the unit, but discovered an abandoned Bristol Bombay aircraft at Chateau-Bouigan and accompanied by fifteen soldiers aboard, flew to England.

On landing in Britain, he claimed to be a fighter pilot and joined the Free French Air Force on 9th September 1940, under the name of Moses Morlaix. Following training at 5 Operational Training Unit, he re-joined No. 1 Squadron, this time as a pilot. He soon began to make a name for himself by quickly shooting down a number of enemy aircraft. His first victim being a Junkers Ju88, which he claimed damaged on 8th November 1940.

He was promoted to the rank of flight commander and awarded the Distinguished Flying Cross in March 1941. He was then posted to 242 Squadron in June 1941, but his stay with them was only brief although he claimed two Messerschmitts destroyed on consecutive days of 22nd and 23rd June. In July, he was again posted this time to No. 91 Squadron based at Hawkinge; here he was credited on 17th July with the sinking of a German minelayer. Early in 1942 he ended his first tour and was posted to No. 11 Group Headquarters. He returned for a second tour with 91 Squadron in June 1942, this time becoming their commanding officer and awarded a Bar to his DFC. By the end of that year, he was to receive the Distinguished Service Order medal. He was promoted to wing commander and returned to serve at 11 Group HQ in December.

In February 1943, Demozay was sent to North Africa to form a flying school for Free French pilots. He returned to London in April 1944 to the French Air Ministry and was told he was to go on a special Mission to Russia.

Following the invasion of France, he formed the Groupment 'Patrie' in France with a variety of aircraft and pilots from the Middle East, operating against German garrisons in by-passed coastal ports. In December 1944, he was awarded the Legion d'Honneur. At war's end, Demozay became deputy commander of all flying training schools in France on 24th October 1945. Tragically, on 19th December his aircraft crashed on route to London and he was killed. Demozay was also awarded the Ordre de Liberation, Croix de Guerre, US DFC, Croix de Guerre (Belgium) and the Czech War Cross. His total score of enemy aircraft destroyed and damaged stood at 18 destroyed and 4 damaged.

Wing Commander Raymond Hiley Harries DSO* DFC**

Harries was born in South Wales in 1916, and was studying as a medical student at Guys Hospital on the outbreak of war in September 1939. He joined the Royal Air Force and on completing his training was posted to No. 43 Squadron based in Scotland. It was here that his only encounter with the enemy took place, at night with a German bomber, but with no success.

He was posted to 52 OTU at Debden in Essex as an instructor. He eventually returned to operational flying in February 1942, becoming a flight commander with 131 Squadron. Here he claimed a number of Focke Wulf fighter aircraft destroyed and damaged. In August he received the award of the DFC. Harries remained with this unit until December and was then posted as commander of 91 Squadron.

On 20th January 1943, in a very ambitious attack, a large formation of Focke Wulf and Messerschmitt fighter bombers attacked London at around midday. The attack was a complete surprise to the RAF, but twelve Spitfires of 91 Squadron were able to intercept the raiders before they dropped their bombs on South London. Ray Harries had been testing out a new throat microphone at West Malling aerodrome, when he heard of the attack. He immediately took off and headed for Beachy Head as the raiders headed for home. As he crossed the coast, he sighted four Messerschmitt 109Gs and attacked them. He shot one down into the sea and probably destroyed another before he himself was attacked in turn by four Focke Wulfs. Harries turned his aircraft into a tight turn and attacked them, damaging one of them before breaking-away and returning home. In April 1943, the squadron received the new Spitfire XIIs powered by the new Griffon engine.

In June, Harries was awarded a Bar to his DFC, the following month his squadron moved to Westhampnett to join No.41 Squadron to form a Spitfire XII Wing. It was while operating from here that Harries claims of enemy aircraft mounted, which brought him promotion as a Wing Leader that August and the following month the award of a second Bar to his DFC and by November the award of the DSO. At the end of December, he was taken off operations and embarked on a tour of the United States of America to lecture on tactics.

On his return to Britain in the spring of 1944, he was given the role of Wing Leader of 135 Wing in the 2nd Tactical Air Force, which operated over France. He was sent on a conversion course in January 1945 on Hawker Tempest aircraft, as his Wing was about to convert over to this type. He was given command of this Wing, but was then posted as Wing Commander Training at 84 Group, 2nd TAF and remained with them until the war ended. He was awarded a Bar to his DSO and also awarded the Croix de Guerre by both the French and Belgian governments.

Ray Harries remained in the RAF after hostilities had ended and became commanding officer of No. 92 Squadron in November 1949. On 14th May 1950, he became lost in bad weather over Liverpool Bay and was killed whilst attempting to bale-out of his Meteor jet aircraft. His final wartime tally for enemy aircraft stood at 15 and 3 shared destroyed. 5 and 1 shared damaged.

Squadron Leader Johnannes Jacobus Le Roux DFC**

Le Roux was born in South Africa in 1920 and was educated in Springs, Transvaal. He worked as an apprentice in the Springs Mines, saving enough money to make a visit to the United Kingdom. Earlier, he and a friend had tried to join the South African Air Force, but had been rejected due to the Air Force's small budget at that time. Having arrived in Britain, they both joined the RAF in February 1939. It has been suggested that on completion of training that Le Roux was posted to a Fairey Battle Squadron in France, but no details are known. He was wounded in France during May 1940, spending six weeks in hospital. On his recovery, he became an instructor near Chester for a short while. In February 1941, he was posted to No. 91 Squadron and promoted to a Flying Officer in that April; became a flight commander during September and was awarded the DFC. He claimed six enemy aircraft destroyed by the end of that year. He finished his tour in December and was sent as an instructor to 55 OTU and remained there until March 1942, after which he was sent to Rolls Royce.

He re-joined No. 91 Squadron as a supernumerary in September 1942, during which he claimed two more victories in the following month and was awarded a Bar to his DFC. Le Roux was posted to North Africa in January 1943 to join 111 Squadron, which he took command of on 26th and led throughout the rest of the Tunisian Campaign until 30th April. During this period, he claimed several more victories. He received a second Bar to his DFC and became a flight controller. He started his third tour of operations in July 1944, when he was given command of 602 Squadron in France. During this time he claimed two Focke Wulf 190s and a Me109, he was also involved in the strafing of a staff car in which it was claimed that German Feldmarschall Erwin Rommel had been travelling; Rommel suffered a fractured skull in the attack, which removed him as Army Commander on the Western Front. Sadly on 29th August 1944, Le Roux took off from landing ground B-19 to fly to England in bad weather, but failed to arrive and was reported as missing. His final wartime victories stood at 18 destroyed 2 probables and 8 damaged.

INDEX

People:

More books available from Mitor Publications

  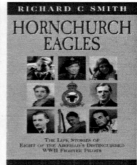

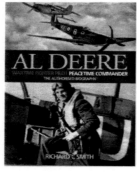 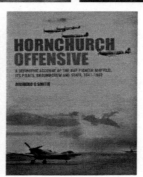

Sergeant Aces of 1940 - Hardback - £15.00
Memories of the Few - Hardback - £15.00
Hornchurch Eagles - Hardback - £12.00
Al Deere - Hardback - £12.00
Hornchurch Offensive - Paperback - £9.99

Prices include postage & packing

Cheques/Postal orders to:
Mitor Publications
20 Theydon Gardens,
Rainham,
Essex
RM13 7TU

For payment by Paypal/Bank Transfer contact: www.mitorpublications.co.uk